# Different Types of Kayaking

ISBN :
1735723312

W0009942

When I first started teaching in 2009, of all the students' questions only one was asked during every class: "What do I do when my boat flips?" Knowing that during the course of the lesson that scary topic would be explained I asked them to hold off until we got there. I learned, though, that scared meant distracted and I learned to talk about it sooner rather than later.

We talk about best practices – blow three long blasts on the whistle attached to your life jacket, float on your back and point your feet down river, etc. Instead of the answer reassuring them, though, the fear I heard behind the question, and those that followed, seemed out of proportion to many capsizes I saw on paddles.

Problem was I was too close to the issue. I related their question to an event that goes something like this - boat flips, paddler swims or walks to the riverbank while the other paddlers grab gear floating downstream. I eventually learned that students imagined themselves trapped under their kayak, or floating helplessly out of control in a churning current and getting slammed into rocks. The problem was that I know kayaking comes in different flavors, but *they didn't*. Many of them thought kayaking is paddling in rapid currents. Period.

Now our classes begin with a brief explanation of the different types of kayaking and classification of waterways, that the lesson covers recreational paddling only and not the high-risk type of kayaking known as "whitewater." That eases the worried looks.

I was curious as to what caused so many of them to think "kayaking" meant the high thrill whitewater stuff.

"The Olympics."

Oh.

"YouTube."

The purpose of this book is to cover the most general basic facts of recreational kayaking based on the author's twenty years of kayaking with groups and twelve as a kayak instructor. If you know little to nothing about kayaking and looking for a book that will get you off to a good start, this one is a great choice. The savings in time and money on buying the correct gear the first time will more than pay for the cost of the book.

Please note that the book covers generalities and not exceptions. There are always exceptions but listing them distracts from discussing most common practices and waters down the writing.

Oh, that, too.

"The news."

It's a wonder any of them showed up for class.

## Water Classifications

The classification of waterways known as The International Scale of River Difficulty enables paddlers worldwide to speak the same language regarding water current. Waterways are categorized on a scale of I-VI, with I being the slowest and easiest to maneuver and VI extremely dangerous to navigate.

A Class I river in Florida has the same characteristics as a Class I river in Germany. Recreational paddling, the subject of this book, takes place in Class I-II current. Only recently has Class VI, once defined as "unkayakable" earned a new description from impossible to kayak to "unraftable." Leave it to fellow kayakers with never-say-die verve earning Class VI this new perspective.

Class I represents the most accessible waterways for new paddlers with obstacle-free calm and lazy rivers. In states with mostly flat terrain, Class I is not much more than floating and navigating. In states with hills, there exists dangers such as downfall, strainers and sieves (defined in Chapter 2) and unsafe for paddlers with no experience. In that case, begin on lakes on wind-free days to build kayaking strength and then go on Class I waterways.

Class II requires a bit more skill to navigate boulders, higher drops of the terrain than covered in Class I, downed trees and other challenges in the waterway.

Waterways change from one classification to a higher one dependent on rain. For a couple days after a severe storm, a creek with no more than a trickle of water transforms into a bank-overflowing Class II-IV. Also, patches of difficult runs on rivers qualify adding "+" or "-" to that river's classification. The photo is an example of a Class II river with a section that is not quite Class III but qualifies for a classification of Class II+:

Whitewater classification begins with Class III. Paddlers *must* know how to self-rescue, perform bombproof rolls and have advanced paddling skills to navigate rapids, standing waves, rocks and

boulders.

Olympic events are performed in Class III-IV whitewater

or, an even better descriptive name, "wildwater."

Class IV waterways are boiling, frothy, raging rivers and

the highest class most kayakers attempt to paddle. The most

violent and dangerous are Classes V and VI.

In my neck of the woods, 'whitewater' is the preferred term for Class III and higher earning its name from the frothy bubbles generated by turbulence. On national on-line message boards, paddlers type "WW" as an abbreviation homogenizing the difference between the terms white- and wildwater.

TIP: Stick to Class I waterways to learn to kayak.

# Types of Kayaking

**Recreational:** Recreational kayaking is the fastest growing type of paddling. There simply are more available waterways at this level and the majority of people prefer it. The slower pace offers more opportunity for viewing wildlife and scenery, is age and gender-neutral meaning boys and girls about age eight through eighty enjoy it, and combines fun with a great workout.

Class I offers smooth, easy paddling depending on where you live. You may encounter winds blowing across a lake that take a little effort to keep the boat moving in a straight line or some tricky bends on a river. In states with flat land, there is not much on the waterways that requires skill. In states with land elevation and rolling hills, as mentioned earlier, Class I can have dangerous features that require skill and muscle. Class II differs from Class I in that you *will* encounter situations that require skill and experience such as "strainers" which look like beaver dams that span horizontally across the water and pulls the current (and you!) toward it, "drop offs" where the terrain suddenly lowers in elevation causing the water to rush and "riffles" or "swifts" which are sections of shallow fast flowing water over a stretch of rocks and boulders. Even lakes advance from Class I to Class II when wind causes whitecaps and waves.

Due to the higher degree of safety, recreational paddling in Class I water is one of the few sports in which families can participate together. Paddle with a group or with a partner. Lots of paddlers even bring their dog.

Another reason for recent popularity is the affordable cost. Recreational kayaks range from $200 for a no-frills floating barge to an elite kayak priced at $900+. Compare this to a whitewater kayak, the cost of which can be twice that of an elite recreational kayak. Purchase a life jacket, paddle and drybag and for a range of $500 to $1,200 you are set up for years of kayaking fun. With care and nothing more mechanical than foot pegs, repairs are minimal.

Recreational kayaking offers multiple opportunities for adventures. Fish in weedy spots inaccessible to larger watercraft, paddle primitive sections of rivers too shallow for motorboats or silently glide near wildlife for great photographs. Stash a tent, change of clothes, food and water in your boat and go river camping. River campers float, for instance, fifteen to twenty miles, stop, camp overnight on the riverbank and then paddle the rest of the trip to the "take-out," the place where the car awaits. This requires a little preplanning to get the cars where they need to be when the paddle is done. Several friends of mine travel to South Florida every year for an inexpensive vacation river camping during the week between Christmas and New Year's.

**Whitewater (aka 'Wildwater'):** Beginning with Class III, whitewater beckons to the adventurous, experienced paddler. Key word: Experienced! Before heading out for the challenge, please have more than a few Class I and Class II trips under your paddle and then prepare by learning from an experienced instructor or whitewater enthusiast how to roll, self-rescue, wet exit and perform rescue techniques.

What is a roll? A maneuver powered by trained muscles that uprights your boat when it capsizes with you remaining in the kayak seat. When that fails, the paddler performs a wet exit meaning that, with the boat upside-down, the paddler frees themselves from the boat and swims to safety.

In the slower waters of Class I, paddlers easily assist one another when anyone flips their boat. Assisting others in Class II is more challenging and rescue practice is recommended. In Class III and higher, self-rescue and group rescue training is a must. ACA and other paddle sport organizations offer courses that teach effective rescue methods. A reliable roll, experienced paddling buds trained in rescues, and the best life jacket and helmet you can afford are the minimum, absolute necessities.

None of this is meant to scare anyone from doing Class III or higher. For the daredevils and adrenaline junkies, the above paragraphs may even entice you. Since this book's audience is paddling novices, understanding the difference between whitewater and recreational paddling especially as it applies to safety is crucial.

Now for the whitewater fun: Skimming along the current, flipping and then righting your kayak, a challenge as accessible as the nearest run, testing your limit, reading the water, ferrying across the river, eddy hopping - it makes doing 3.7 seconds on a bull named Foo Man Choo nothing more than a warm up exercise!

**Ocean (aka 'Surf'):** Ocean and fishing kayaking are close seconds as popular types of kayaking. Companies pump money into engineering new and better designs of ocean kayaks for three reasons: In the sports world, ocean kayaking is new (began in the '70's compared to kayaking in general that is thousands of years old), folks that hang out at the beach generally have more disposable income, and the multiple opportunities for fun that ocean kayaking offers such as fishing or riding the waves.

Nearly every type of kayak has an ocean counterpart. For example, short sea kayaks appear similar to whitewater boats,

and long ones appear similar to touring kayaks. At a glance, I cannot determine the difference between a river and ocean sit-on-top and can imagine that hooking a big one in the ocean means a hootin' and hollerin' free ride until the fish tires and gets pulled onto the deck. Sit-on-tops (SOT) have less of a learning curve than other kayaks. They look like floating waffles. When you capsize, flip the boat upright, climb back on and the water drains through the scupper holes which are openings on the deck through which water drains. The sea kayaks similar to whitewater and touring require more advanced skills.

If riding waves beckons, consider the new "waveski," an elite breed of kayak that come equipped with fins, footstraps, seat and seatbelt.

**Creeking:** Most similar to whitewater but different enough to deserve its own classification. We generally observe creeks as meandering thin ribbons of flowing water that add selling points to a home owner's property. However, due to their narrow channels, it takes one good rainstorm to turn the meandering ribbon into a widened swath of torrential flow. Expect sudden drops and crops of rocks that require so much boat navigating hip action that it would make a belly dancer jealous. As with whitewater kayaking, purchase a helmet and life jacket as though your life depended on it. Creeking can offer some crazy and thrilling rides!

There are kayaks designed specifically designed for creeking. To the uninitiated, these kayaks appear identical to whitewater boats.

**Touring (aka 'Expedition'):** You may want to consider touring kayaking if the thought of paddling long stretches of water and camping along the banks of a river sound appealing. Some of those seen paddling in the ocean are the longest and narrowest of kayaks requiring expert balance and reliable rolls.

John Guider, author of "*A River Inside,*" set off in his backyard creek near Nashville, Tennessee with not much more than his canoe and, at his friend's insistence, an axe. By the end of three months he paddled all the way to New Orleans. He returned home (by land) with the seed of his book, amazing photographs and the desire to do it again. Although Mr. Guider experienced his adventure in a canoe, a touring kayak would work just as good.

Getting away from it all is a good motivator for many touring paddlers. Think of the kayak as a floating cabin in which is stored everything needed for overnighters. Please take a really good first aid kit and know how to use it since you'll be on your own miles from civilization where cell phones towers often do not reach. Better yet, take a buddy or three.

Touring kayaks are most similar to recreational kayaks. The differences will be covered in Chapter 3.

**Slalom racing:** An Olympic event, literally. Competitive slalom kayaking (and canoeing) events are performed in whitewater boats in Class III+ rivers.

Other forms of kayaks include pedal, multi-hull and hybrid boats that blend features of a kayak and canoe sometimes called a kay-oe or canak.

# CHAPTER TWO

# How to Talk Like a Paddler

The following is *not* an index. To better understand the rest of the book, it makes sense to familiarize readers with the words that will be used in the chapters that follow. Besides, indexes are boring and some of what you are about to read is written tongue-in-cheek and hopefully entertaining.

*Bilge pump* - Used to remove water from inside the boat. The best ones simultaneously suck up and propel the water over the

side of the boat. That how the one pictured works. "Super soakers" children water squirt guns will do the job, too, and are great for self- defense during water fights.

*Blade* – used interchangeably for a kayak "paddle."

*Boat camping* - Similar in meaning to "car camping" such that the words 'boat' and 'car' denote method of transporting the gear and do not denote the venue of the campsite. Boat camp on public islands or riverbanks. Canoes and touring kayaks provide ample storage space to stash camping supplies. Recreational kayaks can be outfitted to carry minimum camping needs – sleeping bag, change of clothes, water and food.

*Bow* – Front end of the boat. The back end is the stern. Here's how to easily remember them: B (bow) comes before S (stern).

*Broached* – See "*Pinned*"

*Bulkhead* - An upright seal behind the seat that provides water resistant storage in the rear of the kayak and an air pocket for lift. Either built-in, or added as an option, into a kayak. Strongly recommended for recreational paddlers. Without a bulkhead, an overturned kayak will sink. For real.

*Clamshell* – When a canoe or thin-hulled kayak get pinned by the current against a strainer, the craft will bend in the middle (where the paddler sits) and fold. Life threatening situation.

*Coaming* – Curled down rim around the cockpit over which a spray skirt is attached. We use it to grab the boat for lifting and exiting.

*Cockpit* – The hole where the seat is located. Cockpits come in a large variety of sizes. If you're terrified of getting stuck in a kayak when it's upside down, choose one with a large cockpit and you'll literally fall out when the boat flips.

*Deadfall* – Natural debris in the river such as trees

*Divorce kayak* – (slang) A tandem, two-seater boat. For boaters who understand that the person in front sets the lead for strokes and the person in back does the steering, this term does not apply. If, however, two people paddling together results in banging each other's blades while making little progress in the forward movement through the water, or worse, flips, then this humorous term applies.

*Drops* – Where the land's elevation slopes down resulting in water rushing downhill. On approach, drops sound like waterfalls and will make your stomach lurch, your feet grow cold and you'll say bad words to yourself. But you can do it!

*Drybag* – An indispensable kayaker need. Bags of varying material, size and quality made specifically to keep things inside of it dry. On a small and economical scale, small plastic bags that seal airtight are drybags. Fold the top down twice then clip, snap or buckle it shut. Despite that instructions say to burp it, leave air inside when closing it to provide buoyancy in the event of a capsize. The best size for moving water is a small/5 liter. For slower water, medium/10 liter. Get a bright color so you can find it when (not if) you capsize.

*Edging* – A polished method of making the boat glide around a curve. Although one can edge while recreational kayaking, it is primarily a whitewater term that refers to slightly tilting the boat up by pushing down one hip, thigh or knee while continuously paddling and keeping your head centered.

*Emergency blanket* – Metal-colored shiny thin plastic that comes in a small pouch that opens to the size of a shower curtain. Reflects body heat back to the person around whom iti s wrapped. Used for hypothermia, shock. If a paddler capsizes and the air or water, or both, are cold, don't wait until the paddler starts shaking to take action. The paddler need to undress, towel dry and get wrapped the emergency blanket. Ask them to dress while covered in the blanket so no skin is exposed.

*Feathered* – Refers to angling paddle blades 45, 60 or 90 degrees. Most recreational paddling is done with the blades straight up and down. When paddling in the wind, however, the feathered blade slices through the breeze.

*Life Jacket* – Those made specifically for kayaking are short in the back which prevents them from touching the seat and rising up around your ears. If your height is at least 6'1" ignore this – you can wear the life jackets with longer backs. Summer life jackets are open on the sides. Winter ones are made of neoprene, much like the ones worn by scuba divers. Ladies, if you have large flotations (that's why my students call them), purchase a life jacket that goes over your head. These have open sides which prevents chafing.

*Long boat* - (slang) A kayak that is not used for whitewater.

*Long boaters* – (slang) A term used by whitewater paddlers to differentiate their flavor of kayaking from those who paddle recreational kayaks. Recreational paddlers do *not* call themselves long boaters.

*Noodle arms* – (slang) This condition sneaks up on you the day after paddling. Your worn-out muscles make your arms so sore that they're limp for a couple days. If this happens, there is only one reason why: You aren't paddling the correct way. The correct method is coming up in Chapter 5.

*Outfitter* – Our best friends, most of whom are waterfront, who own businesses of renting kayak and canoes. In many states, these seasonal businesses rely on a few months of business to pay twelve months of bills. They're a great resource and help with questions about their waterways. They are the gateway through which many people walked until they became boat owners. Tip them well.

*Paddle* – Also known as 'blade.' Used as a verb (Let's go paddle!), noun (Put your paddle in the water). Add an "r" to the end and it becomes a common noun (Are you a paddler?).

*Paddle float* – Also known as 'outrigger.' Flotation devices that encase paddle blades for the purpose of balancing the boat in

 much the same way that training wheels balance a bicycle. Paddle floats can also be purchased that do not attach to the paddle blade but, instead, attach to the boat as a separate device. Used for rescues, to balance a boat while fishing or to create a "barge" kayak for camping.

*Paddle leash* – A stretchy cord that, with one end clipped onto the boat (or the paddler) and the other around the paddle, tethers the paddle to the boat or paddler and prevents paddle loss. Do not use these on waterways that include strainers, downhill slopes or intermittent fast-moving water - they pose a dangerous entrapment risk in the event of a capsize.

*Pillow* – Water flowing downstream over a rock. On approach, it could look like a good place to paddle over but it is not. Generally, a whitewater term.

*Pinned* (also called *"broached*)– A dangerous situation when a boat gets trapped sideways to the current against a tree, debris or rock. It also refers to a paddler who is out of their kayak and pummeled so vigorously by the current against an object that they cannot move. If the boat has a thin hull, pinning results in a crushed and/or submerged kayak. If you cannot immediately free the boat, abandon it. A pinned paddler is in immediate life-threatening danger.

*Point* – The lead paddler of a group who is experienced reading water, looks out for potential danger spots and scouts best navigation on the waterway. All other paddlers stay behind the Point. If there are experienced canoeists among the group, their higher elevation in the water as opposed to kayaks makes them ideal Point paddlers.

*Portage* – A fancy word for carrying or pulling your boat. Perhaps the water is too low to float the kayak, an object such as a low-lying tree blocks the river or current is beyond the paddler's experience level. Paddlers also shorten it to "port." Note: pronounced "port ij" or "por tahj."

*Put-in* – A spot where paddlers begin a paddle, often at a bridge or boat ramp.

*Rack* – (slang) Short for 'roof rack.'

*Rec* – Short for 'recreational' kayak, as in, "Nice rec boat."

*Recreational kayak* – Most defining features is its large cockpit. Range in size from ten to fourteen feet. Built for stability and, in the higher price range, comfort and good tracking. Disadvantages: Longer boats do not take curves as good as shorter boats. Thin inexpensive rec boats put paddlers at risk when confronting dangerous river conditions such as strong currents and strainers. (See *"Pinned" or "Strainers"*)

*Riffles* – A short stretch of the river characterized by shallow water and a long stretch of rocks. The water looks sparkly or bubbly as it runs over these rocks. The danger of riffles is the sudden increased water velocity. Riffles can be seen and not heard, as opposed to drops which can be heard on approach.

*Roll* – A whitewater term referring to the act of righting a kayak after a capsize. For example: Eskimo roll. Recreational kayaks are not made for rolls, but possible in one in which the rider's hips touch both sides and with the boat skirted. (see *"Skirt"*)

*Rudder* – A device that, like a dog's tail, flips up over the back of the boat (stern) and lowers into the water, the movement of which is controlled by the paddler's feet. It's usually an added purchase for a kayak. The rudder assists the boat moving straight or as a passive use for rounding curves using the current's momentum. It saves energy as the paddler does not have to use as much effort to keep the boat moving straight. It's recommended for windy lakes, deep rivers and ocean paddles. Remember: Flip the rudder up when in shallow water.

*Run* – (slang) Synonym for the verb 'paddle': "We're going for a run on the river."

*Run the chute* – (slang) As the result of obstructions such as rocks or downed trees, the downstream current splits around the obstructions. These separate currents are called chutes. From upstream, a paddler must decide which chute looks the best. The decision begins with a few minutes of holding the kayak still in the water, or scanning from the land, for the best chute to run.

*SOT* – Sit-on-top kayak

*Sculling* – Moving the paddle in the water in a figure '8'. Used to maintain stability, as a draw stroke to move the boat sideways or by whitewater paddlers to resurface a capsized kayak.

*Self-bailing* – This does not refer to the paddler as the 'self' in self-bailing. It refers to a feature of the boat; more specifically to SOT scupper holes that allow water to drain from the boat.

*Self-rescue* – Depending upon one's self for up-righting and re-entry. Self-rescue is associated with paddling Class III+ bodies of water.

*Shuttle, non-shuttle paddle* – On a shuttle paddle the put-in and take-out are geographically distant from one another. Beginning at one bridge on a river and paddling downstream to another bridge is an example of a shuttle paddle. Shuttle paddles require at least two vehicles as one is left at the put-in and the other at the take-out. Some state parks as well as outfitters offer shuttle services. Non-shuttle paddles begin and end at the same place. Lone paddlers can do non-shuttle paddles by paddling upriver x number of miles and then drifting back downstream.

*Sieve* – See *Strainer*

*Sit-on-top* – SOT. Also known as *sit upons*. Multiple uses - for recreational, whitewater and sea kayaking. Advantages: Easy to mount as there is no cockpit to climb inside, foot rests molded into the boat, scupper holes for self-draining, after a capsize paddler flips boat and climbs back on, full open deck allows for more gear storage. Disadvantages: No back rest, paddler stays in same seated position for duration of trip, higher center of gravity that may result in less stability (does not apply to all sit-on-tops, some manufacturers compensate with lower seats), generally slower moving than sit insides.

*Skeg* – With the kayak suspended, turned sideways and the skeg down, it looks like a tongue sticking out from the bottom of the boat. Some are not and some are retractable.  Its use is more for compensating for the wind rather than tracking, a definite plus for lake and sea kayaking.

*Skirt* – Full name is spray skirt. An apparel/device that seals one's body to a whitewater kayak for the purpose of preventing water from entering the boat. Used with Class III+. For recreational kayaks, half skirts are available that fit around the front half of the cockpit (only) decreasing the size of the cockpit by 50% in the event of rain or turbulent water.

*Slice* – Holding the paddle at an angle as it enters the water instead of straight up and down.

*Strainer* – These look like beaver dams on the water, a cluster of limbs, branches and dead trees. Water flows through them but we do not. Even small ones direct the current to flow toward it. When a paddler gets caught in that current, it forces their kayak into the debris which is an immediate life-threatening situation. Sieves are underwater strainers.

*Swamped* – A water-filled kayak.

*Sweep* – The last person in a group paddle on a waterway. All paddlers should remain behind the Point and in front of the Sweep. The Sweep should be the strongest paddler in the group because they are the last line of defense to swoop downstream to assist with a capsize. As such, they might have to work alone until others paddle upstream to assist.

*Swimmer* – (slang) Also called "Floater." Navy folks would call out, "Man overboard!" A swimmer is a capsized paddler.

*Take-out* – The end location of a paddle.

*Tandem* – Boat with two or more seats. Recreational, touring, whitewater and sit-on-tops are all available as tandems.

*Touring kayak* – These boats track like a dream and the length provides plenty of stowing space for camping equipment as they have two bulkheads. They range from thirteen to much longer. Pros: They effectively cover long distances with less effort compared to a rec kayak making them a great choice for lakes. Cons: They are a bugger to make quick turns. Because they're narrow, they also flip more easily than a rec boat.

*Tracking* – How straight the boat stays with each paddle stroke. Good tracking = the boat stays straight. Bad tracking = the boat points first in one direction then the other with each stroke. The longer the boat, the better it tracks. An 8' boat cannot compare to a 12' boat for tracking while neither compares to the tracking ability of a 17' touring kayak.

*WW* – paddler's abbreviation for whitewater or wildwater

*Yak* – (slang) Kayak

*Note: This list is not comprehensive, and lists primarily terms found in this book for recreational kayakers.*

# CHAPTER THREE

# Types of Kayaks

In the broadest sense, there are two types of kayaks: Sit inside and sit on top (SOT).

Sit inside kayaks                    Sit on top kayaks

**Recreational:** While many paddlers use SOTs for recreational kayaking, for the purpose of this book let's agree that recreational kayaking is done in sit inside kayaks to give more clarity to the discussion.

A defining feature of a recreational kayak is the large cockpit as opposed to the much smaller one found on a touring kayak. That's how to tell at a glance whether the boat is a recreational or touring kayak.

A recreational river paddler's best friends are weight (of the boat) and length. Recreational boats range from eight to fourteen feet in length, and from thirty-two to seventy plus pounds. Avoid the low and high ranges of these lengths and weights. Most paddlers find that the perfect length for recreational kayaks is ten to twelve feet with a weight in the forties. Choose a twelve-footer if you are taller than five feet five inches.

If the boat is too light with a weight in the thirty-something pound range, it floats on top of the water as opposed to *in* the water which makes it difficult to make it go where you want it to go. Imagine putting a plastic bowl in a swimming pool. With a light flick of the wrist the bowl swirls around. In terms of being on a river, that flick of the wrist mimics the action of a good wind or the current. Now imagine a heavier soup bowl in the pool. It sits deeper in the water as it isn't as buoyant as the lighter plastic – it displaces water which is a good thing in that it contributes to stability.

Durability is another issue. Consider that the difference between a forty-five and a thirty-two pound boat is thirteen pounds of whatever material of which the boat is made. The denser the boat, the longer it stands up to gouges, dings and dragging.

Bottom line: The shorter and lighter boats are less stable and durable than longer and heavier ones. In anything much more than lakes, they're less safe, too. For ladies concerned about carrying a longer and heavier boat, we'll cover tips in Chapter 7 how to load and unload a kayak. I know from experience leading groups that loading a kayak on a car is a really.big.deal. for women. You're going to learn a method that takes away the heavy lifting. I promise.

Of all sit inside kayaks, rec boats are the ones built for stability. The long pencil-thin boats you may have seen racing are twenty-three or less inches wide while a rec is twenty-seven to thirty-fourinches wide. The width is a function of length.

Racing Kayak

Recreational kayak

The long, narrow touring boats are 'tippy' while the wider recs are more stable. But the downside of wider kayaks is decreased tracking. A twelve feet a recreational kayak offers both stability and good tracking, dependent on the manufacturer.

TIP: I once paddled a thirty-two inch wide boat and continually banged the paddle against the sides because it was just too wide to clear with each stroke.

If you are really tall (6'3"+), it seems logical to choose a short paddle, with 210 cm. considered short. However, the opposite is true. Tall people should choose a longer than average paddle (240 cm). Here's why: If a tall person uses a short paddle, they'll lift it higher in the air to reach the water and get water on them and in the kayak. A longer paddle allows tall kayakers to easily and more effectively reach the water when utilizing long strokes.

A factor that has an adverse effect on stability is if the seated paddler's hips span the width of the boat. If the paddler is too full in the seat, each wiggle of the paddler's behind causes rocking, unstable movements of the kayak. For whitewater paddling, body contact with the kayak is the goal. For recreational paddling, that doesn't work. We need to be able to move inside our kayaks without our boat responding. If a paddler's hips fill the seat and make contact with the sides of the boat, simply turning the torso causes the boat to dip down to the water. Not good. For safety's sake, encourage wide-bottomed paddlers to begin in canoes instead of kayaks or a hybrid canoe-kayak.

With recreational kayaking, good tracking is everything. Here's the definition for tracking from Chapter 2: "Tracking –

How straight the boat stays with each paddle stroke. Good tracking = the boat stays straight. Bad tracking = the boat points first in one direction then the other with each stroke. The determining factor for tracking is length. The longer the boat, the better it tracks. An eight-foot boot cannot compare to a twelve foot boat for tracking while neither compares to a seventeen foot touring kayak."

A river paddler in an eight-foot boat corrects with *each stroke* the direction the boat points while moving the kayak forward. I've seen an eight-foot boat exhaust a well-toned paddler during a ten-mile trip while others in ten- to twelve-foot boats had way less of a problem.

It's important to match the kayak to the type of waterway. River rats need at the very least ten feet. Twelve is best.

Other than the large opening of the cockpit and ten to fourteen feet lengths, there are no other statements that purely define a recreational kayak.

TIP: Low end boats often have an uncomfortable, butt-numbing molded seat. Buy a stadium cushion or thicker seat for comfort.

**Touring:** Here are some unique features of a touring kayak: length range of thirteen plus feet, small diameter cockpit, streamlined bow and stern.

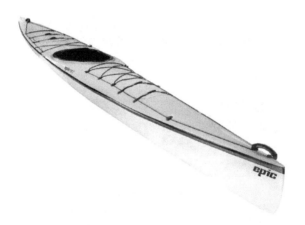

These boats slice through water with little effort because their owner intends to cover long distances, reach top speed, or both. Watching someone glide across a large lake in a touring kayak is like watching music in motion. With the wind at their back, these paddlers zip along the water almost as fast as sailboats.

Synonymous words for touring kayaks are expedition or sea. An expedition tour might be a daylong or overnight excursion or a week of river camping. Due to the greater lengths, these boats offer more hatches, deck rigging and space to stash things like tents, sleeping bags, change of clothing and food.

**Whitewater:** When I first saw a whitewater kayak, I thought it looked like a Dutch wooden shoe:

Photos by Leslie Dunn

Although whitewater boats can be measured in feet, to talk like a real paddler measure by gallons instead with a range of 45-95. The higher the volume, the higher it sits in the water and resurfaces faster. Whitewater boats are "outfitted" which means padding is added to more snugly fit the boat to the paddler. Points of contact gives the paddler control they need to perform the variety of maneuvers to survive whitewater. The net effect of the points of contact is that the whitewater boat becomes an extension of the paddler's body almost like wearing a shoe.

Photo by Leslie Dunn

Pressing down with one leg or hip turns these responsive boats. Push down with one hip while keeping your head in the center of the boat and it lowers on that side; that's "edging."

With a sharp upward jerk of the butt, a "hip snap," the boat responds with an upward thrust to right itself when upside down. In whitewater, capsizing is the norm which makes a quick and effective roll critical. Permitting as little water as possible to get inside the boat is just as critical. To prevent water from getting inside the boat, whitewater boaters wear "skirts." The skirts are water resistant, not waterproof. They fit snugly over the lip, or coaming of the cockpit with the top portion of it literally worn by the paddler. A grab tab is attached to the front of the skirt. When placing the skirt over the coaming, it is essential that the grab tab sticks out. If a paddler finds themself unable to perform an effective roll, a quick yank on the grab tab frees the skirt from the coaming and the kayaker performs a "wet exit." With a thrust of their legs, the paddler, wearing the skirt, clears the boat and swims to safety.

**Special Note:** Do not take a recreational kayak into Class III+ river. Recreational kayaks can be used for Class I and Class II only, and I say Class II with reluctance. I do not recommend any recreational kayak over ten feet for Class II. Class III paddling must be done in a kayak designed specifically for whitewater.

Whitewater kayaks function opposite to that of recreational boats. Here are some of the general differences:

| Whitewater | Recreational |
| --- | --- |
| Nine feet and less | Ten feet and longer |

| | |
|---|---|
| Built to recover from capsizing | Built for stability |
| Snugger fit the better ('outfitted') | Boat wider than paddler |
| Flotation assists | Not necessary |
| Ideal for quick turning | Shaped for going straight |

(There are exceptions to all of these but in the interest of this book these are general guidelines.)

What about taking a whitewater kayak down a Class I or II river? As noted earlier, it's just not a good idea as it exhausts the paddler. What makes it exhausting? Tracking. Think of watching a duck walk away from you and the way it's butt waddles first one way and then the other. That is bad tracking. These short six- to eight-foot whitewater boats perform as designed by responding to each stroke pointing left with a stroke on the right side and then pointing right with a stroke on the left. Conversely in a rec boat with good tracking, the boat stays straight with each stroke. It's worth repeating: In recreational kayaking, good tracking is *everything*. This is a defining difference between recreational and whitewater kayaking. With whitewater, a boat that turns on a dime is crucial.

**Inflatables:** There are so many from which to choose, and at alluring prices. The cheapies cost $100 or less. More durable ones cost over $1,000. When browsing ads, to avoid inadvertently purchasing an inflatable please read the ad thoroughly! Some advertisers bury the word 'inflatable' in the boat description or even avoid the word. Here's an example of a deliberately vague inflatable kayak ad:

"Performance Travel Kayak.... Inflatable seats with adjustable support backrest and mesh pocket." No kayak has inflatable seats except inflatable kayaks.

Inflatables are great additions to camping or bike trips because they can be folded up and stored for a short run. A family can purchase several for the cost of one hard-shell kayak. For a brief three-mile paddle on a Class I river, an inflatable is adequate.

Now for the down side. With wind or water current of anything more than low velocity, an inflatable spins in circles on top of the water to a worse degree than a lightweight kayak. The air inside of it keeps it buoyant and, unless there is some hefty weight inside, it stays on the top of the water like a piece of foam. Inflatables have little to no tracking ability. Paddlers told me that it feels as if the boats have a mind of their own; most strokes will be spent correcting the direction of the boat. I have seen a couple exceptions: a tandem inflatable with two riders who provided enough weight to counteract the inflatable's buoyancy, and a high-end inflatable made of heavy enough material and with a metal spine that lowered the boat into the water such that it provided traction.

When an inflatable springs a leak, the inflatable kayak will be where? On the water. The repair process: Dry the boat. Patch the hole. Dry the patch. During one paddle, a member's inflatable acquired two leaks. Thirty-five people waited an hour with each of the two repairs. On another run, a paddler literally spun in circles in the mild, two mile per hour current. Mid-way through the paddle, the exhausted newbie deflated her boat and hopped into someone's canoe. She later said that she had noodle arms for a couple days.

**Tandem:** A boat with two seats instead of one. Most boats can be purchased as tandems. Tandems are an option for those with a paddle partner or who need an extra seat for a child, pet or gear. Two people who paddle in synch can easily outdistance a solo boat. On a non-shuttled river paddle with half of the run going with and the other half against the current, it's advantageous to have two people who can trade off paddling to prevent fatigue. On the down side, that added seat means extra length and weight. Generally, expect the sixty-pound range and higher for a recreational tandem boat.

Two people who clack each other's paddles and find themselves navigating into the bushes are not having fun. The fix is simple. The rear paddler synchronizes strokes with that of the front paddler, and the rear paddler's role is that of the boat's rudder. The person up front cannot see the person in the back, that's why it is up to the rear paddler to synch up with the front paddler. When the rear paddler matches the front paddler's strokes, the boat zings through the water. I know. I've tried to keep up with them.

One other important thing in *any* two-seater boat is that the heavier person sits in the back. This includes canoes.


**Sit on top (SOT) or Sit Upons:** The advantages of a SOT are: self-draining through scupper holes, in the event of a capsize SOT's are more easily climbed onto as opposed to sit-insides and some so stable that one can stand up while floating on the water. Because of the open deck, paddlers with limited flexibility or long legs feel less confined on a sit on top.

A lengthy sit-on-top outfitted for fishing is a fisherman's (or woman) dream with bait well, netted pockets, built-in rod holders, deck rigging, straps and hatches - everything the fisherman needs within arm's length. Snap that wiggling fish up onto the deck. You couldn't do that in a sit-inside without getting fish whacked.

On the beach, you'll see paddlers on sit-on-tops riding the waves along with the surfers or far from the shore for some fishing.

Disadvantages: Back strain after prolonged sitting, water coming up onto the deck through the scupper holes.

---

# CHAPTER FOUR

# Buying a Kayak and Necessary Gear

With so many makes and models of kayaks on the market, selecting one is like going into a pet store for a puppy. Unless you know what you want, your decision will probably be based on emotion or your favorite color rather than information.

Beginning your kayak years in your own boat gives you the advantage of matching your growing style to the specifications of your kayak, but please ask several seasoned paddlers for some advice before the purchase and do your research.

At the risk of sounding corny, revealing flaws about one's boat, though, is like ratting on a best friend. After using their boat a few times, paddlers forget any shortcomings that they eventually adapted to and asking people if they like their kayak is not a good idea. For example, my new twelve-foot boat was difficult to navigate around sharp bends but I learned how to compensate and no longer consider it an issue. Its stability outperformed any other kayak I'd owned, a factor of greater importance to me than quick turns.

Students who decide to purchase a kayak ask which one is the most versatile, meaning, which kayak can do it all? There is no such thing. A rec kayak made for Class I waterways can be adapted for Class II with a half-skirt and extra flotation, and a whitewater kayak can be taken down a Class I river but that's like using golf clubs to ski. It'll get the job done but expect some issues. A whitewater boat is as different from a touring boat as a race car from a SUV. Using the right boat for the job maximizes the performance of both the boat and the paddler.

When shopping for a boat, here are the primary considerations:

- What type of waterway will you paddle?

- Slow or fast current?

- How often you will kayak – twice a month, twice a season, twice a year?

- How important is the longevity of the boat?

- How much can you afford to spend?

Let's look at some of the must-have's vs the nice-to-have.

**River? Lake? Ocean? – Different boats for different strokes**

Generally speaking, lake kayaking is a paddle of solitude. Recreational paddlers often paddle with groups. Whitewater

Photo by Leslie Dunn

pits man against the force of nature - that's as far as I dare go categorizing paddlers.

By now you may have a better understanding of the type of kayaking in which you are most interested. For the rest of the text referring to boat purchase, this brief list will apply:

Lakes: Length is the primary feature. These are the longest and narrowest boats in the kayaking family.

Class I: For river paddlers, stability is crucial. Although twelve feet is the sweet spot, not all of them are built the same. In my opinion, kayaks manufactured by Perception tip more easily than ones made by Wilderness System. But the Perception zips through the water faster. It depends on what you prefer – stability or speed.

Class II: Nine or ten feet of sit inside or SOT works great.

Class III+: Whitewater kayaks only – six to eight feet long.

Overnighters: Length again, but not to the extreme as lake paddling. Kayaks that are fourteen to seventeen feet in length include two bulkheads that create two hatches for storage.

Ocean: Sit on tops ranging from eight to fourteen feet; also, the long touring boats are often seen in the surf. TIP: If using a touring boat on the ocean, you better know how to effectively roll the kayak.

**Honestly – how often will you kayak?**

Maybe it's premature to ask how often you will kayak if you haven't yet set foot in one. You will know within your first three to five paddles whether or not it's the sport for you.

Renting or borrowing first is a great idea. If outfitters are available in your area, request a kayak of different length and manufacturer with each run. Join a paddle group and ask to borrow boats from members.

TIP: Anytime money exchanges hands, it is not borrowing. It is renting and carries the risk of potential legal issues.

There may be a good reason you cannot own a kayak such as a shortage of storage space. Check if a friend or relative will share a spot in their yard or cellar/basement. Kayaking in your own boat is absolutely the way to go. In the long run it is worth investing an additional couple hundred for a higher quality boat with extra features, especially a padded adjustable seat, a bulkhead and cup holder.

Or you may try kayaking and decide yes, I like it, it's not the best thing I've ever done but I'll do it occasionally. If that's the case, don't purchase the cheapest barge out there or the few trips in it will only strengthen your resolve to end your paddling days. When manufacturers go for inexpensive it is at the expense of maneuverability and comfort and could turn your lukewarm feelings for paddling into downright dislike. The least expensive boats are miserable at tracking and are uncomfortable. If you won't paddle a lot, it's probably best to just rent from a local outfitter for a couple reasons. Outfitters purchase higher quality kayaks meant to last and they choose boats specific for their types of waterways.

### How long will a kayak last?

The two words on which to focus are care and cost. You can purchase a less expensive craft and prolong its usage with good care and, conversely, purchase a more expensive boat but without good care shorten its longevity.

To ensure the endurance of your boat, buy one designed for your favorite kind of kayaking. If you live where the river bottoms are sandy or most of your paddling will be on a lake, consider purchasing a fiberglass boat. That medium drives up the cost but is long lasting and lightweight. If, however, you live where the rivers are rocky, fiberglass will break because it's, well, made of glass. Fiberglass (and Kevlar) boats can be repaired but it's more fun to have your boat in the water than in the repair shop. For bodies of water with rocky bottoms, choose a thicker and durable material such as Rotomold (Rotationally Molded) plastic. Imagine peeling a potato. Those long curls of skin resemble the gouging effect of going over rocks which are unavoidable for river paddlers in many states.

TIP: For boat repairs, check with a boat supply store to see if they repair yaks. Some manufacturers sell patch kits comprised of the same material as the boat for do-it-yourself repairs.

Even when used for the purpose for which they are designed, kayaks take a beating. Sometimes they have to be dragged from the car to the put-in or up a cement boat ramp, across rocky river bottoms when the water is low or portaged through the woods around a dam.

TIP: When transporting from the car to the water without assistance, from paddle to paddle alternate dragging the boat from the stern and bow. Despite continued bilging, water kept collecting inside my kayak during a winter paddle. I asked the group to pull over so I could check it out. I discovered a nasty long gash on the bottom of the stern, the result of eight years of pulling the boat by bow only.

Let's say you are considering purchasing a ten-feet, thirty-two pound kayak that costs $200. At this length, weight and price, the frame can be bent. With moderate paddling at twice a month, this is a one season kayak. At the risk of sounding scary, that one season might not be a safe one in some states for reasons discussed in Chapter 6.

It's reasonable for a top-grade kayak to last ten years or more with good care. What is good care?

- Keep it out of direct sunlight when not in use.

- Rinse off salt water.

- Suspend it for storage as opposed to laying it down.

- Alternate between strapping it face up and face down to transport it.

- Minimal dragging over cement

As with anything else, the more you spend, the higher the quality. With regards to kayaks, as little as $200 *significantly* amps up the quality of the boat. After years of paddling, I still believe that $400 is the minimum for a quality kayak.


**How much can you afford to spend?**

Usually cost is everything but if you are a summer warrior, where you live summers are three months long and you plan to paddle infrequently, even if you can afford an elite kayak spend those hard-earned dollars on other things and purchase a less expensive boat. But if during those three months you will kayak as much as a Floridian would in a year, it would be worth it to get the higher end kayak. Then again, if most of those paddles during the three month summer take place in a lake with little chance of scuffing the bottom of the boat, this would be another reason to not invest in an elite kayak.

The best time to purchase is at the end of season sales. Rec kayaks take up a lot of a store's floor space and managers want them sold. They're also like cars such that each year has its "model." Prices come down as much as $200 making it possible to purchase an elite kayak for the price of a non-elite!

Looking for a used kayak? Here in Nashville, many whitewater boats appear on Craigslist but recreational kayaks are rare. Paddlers marry their boat and give them up only after they are beyond repair. I snapped up a rec boat within hours of the owner posting it on the internet meaning it is possible to find a deal but if waiting to purchase a used boat is holding you back from paddling, rent or borrow until the end of the season sales. The most expensive types of kayaks are touring and whitewater. Some whitewater boats cost as much as $2000 and more.

TIP:  Before purchasing a kayak, consider the size of the paddler and check the boat's minimum and maximum weight limit suggested by the manufacturer. There is an ideal proportion of paddler to kayak – a six foot person in a kayak with a length of ten feet is like trying to cram a size eleven foot into a size nine shoe. Conversely, children and petite women fit nicely, and paddle more effectively, in ten foot recreational crafts.

Consider purchasing a boat with this type of built-in handles:

I've seen this type yank right out of the boat:

and there goes the means by which to carry it.

Nice features to have: Bulkhead, drain plug, cup holder, dry hatch, deck rigging, adjustable seat, foot braces, thigh pads, dashboard.

Special note: Of the 'Nice features to have" for recreational paddlers, the advantages of bulkheads almost puts it into the Must Have features, according to recreational paddlers without one. A bulkhead is an upright wall that reaches side-to-side behind the seat partitioning off nearly a third of the boat, from behind the seat to the stern. Manufacturers use the dry space to equip the kayak with a cargo hatch. When a boat swamps, the bulkhead prevents the stern from filling with water and also provides buoyancy due to the trapped air meaning that the boat will not sink. Plus it creates a nice dry space for storage - not waterproof but water resistant.

**Necessary Equipment**

**Paddle** – The things to consider before purchasing a paddle are type of paddling, size of the paddler and width of the boat. The right paddle for the job, and for you, is as important as the choice of kayak. The paddle is the piston and you are the engine. If you are unsure about what to purchase, borrow other paddles. Finding out what you don't like is as valuable as finding out what you do like.

Paddle variables include length of the shaft, width and shape of the blades, weight and material of both the blades and shaft. Whitewater paddles are the shortest in the paddle family. The blade on a touring paddle is narrower than the blade for recreational paddling. Recreational blades come in a variety of shapes and sizes.

Wide blades provide greater acceleration because they have more surface area to create water resistance, meaning that they are muscle builders. If you plan on long trips, such as expeditions, go for a thinner blade. If you plan lots of river runs, select wider blades.

Weight matters! The cheapest paddles are the heaviest and quickly fatigue even seasoned kayakers. Paddle manufacturers are catching on that women need a smaller diameter shaft.

I bought four paddles before I found the one that suited me best. One of the four was an expensive carbon paddle that weighed as much as a dime. OK, a quarter. But the blades flexed during strokes, I couldn't go fast so I went back to hard plastic.

Occasionally we see bent shaft paddles. They look like the crankshaft of a car. Another rarity is a wooden paddle. These untraditional paddles are great conversation starters and their owners swear by them.

Paddles range from 180 – 240 cm and longer. The taller the recreational paddler or wider the boat, the longer the shaft that's needed.

Drip rings are the two small rubber rings just south of each blade. They're supposed to catch water dripping off the edge of the blade and prevent it from leaking down the shaft. They don't do their job. Period. It gets worse. Within a short amount of time, they dry out and slip down the shaft. Paddlers shift the placement of their hands relative to the location of the drip rings. The net result is that their hands are off-center and the paddler wonders why they can't make their boat go straight. My best advice: Cut off the drip rings because they don't work anyway..

I've seen even experienced yakkers paddle with their paddle upside down. If you paddle with blades of an asymmetric shape, meaning like the photograph below:

ensure that the blade's scoop (also called power face) and manufacturer's name face you. Most companies print their company's name on the side of the blade facing the paddler, and most print it such that the print lies horizontal to the shaft. If the company's name looks upside down, so is the paddle.

**Gloves** – There are two ways to paddle which we'll cover in Chapter 5 but if you are like most folks, you pull on the paddle instead of push.

You can tell how someone paddles – if they wear gloves, they are a 'pull' paddler which causes blisters and why gloves is in the required section of this text. Paddler gloves are made to get wet and cover only one-third of the length of our fingers. I prefer the type with Velco straps around the wrists. To prevent mildew and get rid of stanky river odors, toss the gloves in the washer with your laundry.

If you paddle during cold weather, wear full-fingered gloves made of neoprene.

**Dry bag** – A dry bag is a must. Two small ones are recommended over one large for paddlers on moving water; the small are large enough to hold everything I carry including a digital SLR camera. When a boat is moving swiftly downstream, there simply is no time to dig through a large drybag. Note: The thick plastic transparent ones, in my experience, do not last as long as the vinyl ones.

What goes into drybags on a paddle? Sunscreen, insect repellent, poncho/raincoat, knife, lighter or waterproof matches, first aid kit and anything that might be hard to replace in the event of a capsize such as car keys, glasses, etc.

TIP: Purchase a drybag made of a bright color such as yellow or red. The dark blue and green ones can be difficult to spot when someone capsizes.

**Life Jacket** – Buy a Type III life jacket with a generous cut to the armholes and *shortened back* designed for paddlers. Nice features to shop for: women's cut for ladies, mesh for summer, neoprene for colder months.

Nice comfortable summer life jacket

Do not buy the U-shaped ones typically seen on motorboats as the one pictured below. Because of its length, the bottom of it will rest against your lap and seat and travel up around your ears.

Make sure the life jacket is adjustable and correct size. Some use the standard S, M, L; some utilize chest size in inches. Try it on before you buy. Imagine someone grabbing you by the shoulder strap to pull you out of the water. That's how to make sure that it fits snug enough that you won't slip from inside of it.

TIP: Don't store anything in the life jacket pockets. Trust me, those zippers open by themselves while paddling and there goes your car keys. It's happened more than once.

**Whistle** – I call it your cell phone to 911 in the event of a flip. Attach one end of it to a lanyard or string and the other end to your life jacket. Don't get plastic – it breaks the first time you sit on it. Don't get steel – it rusts. Get aluminum.

TIP: If using string, measure the distance from waist to mouth, and add a couple inches for knots. Keep it at this length to prevent it from potentially wrapping around your neck while in the water. Also, please do not attach anything else to the outside of the life jackert. Precious time is lost fumbling through dangling belongings when grabbing the whistle during an emergency.

**River shoes** – If you paddle on waterways with sandy bottoms, flip flops work. If you paddle on waterways with rocky bottoms, wear waterproof shoes that Velcro, tie or even rubber ankle boots. Nothing ruins the day more than an uncomfortable kayak seat or the teeny rocks in your river shoes. If you wear sneakers on rivers with tiny ground-up rocks, you'll end up barefoot because everything gets in them and nothing comes out.

These for winter paddles:

**Bilge pump** – Even without a capsize, water manages to find its way into kayaks. It may dribble down the paddle, drip off shoes or as the

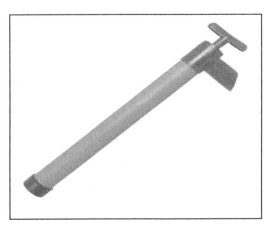

result of a fun water gun fight. If it rains during the paddle, that wide cockpit on recreational boats permits lots of rain to get inside. Or you may have unexpectedly run into a Class II section of the river and taken on some water from standing waves. Forget something as simple as a sponge. We take on a little too much water for that to be of good use. Every paddler must carry a device of some kind that removes water quickly and more efficiently than a sponge. As this device removes water from the inside of the boat it simultaneously pumps the water out over the side of the boat. Even boats with drain plugs retain some water that must be bilged.

**Optional Equipment**

**Dog leash** – Old paddler's trick for portaging the kayak. When the water is too shallow to paddle or there's an obstruction too dangerous to paddle through, clip the leash on the boat's handle on the front or back to pull it.

**Seat pad** – Recreational kayakers spend hour after hour sitting in one position. Unless the kayak has a padded seat, bring along some extra cushioning including lumbar support if you need it.

**Paddle floats** ("outrigger") – like training wheels they stabilize the kayak. Also used for rescues or to create a carry-all barge kayak if you're doing an overnighter on flat water such as an island on a large lake.

**Wetsuit** – Although listed in the optional equipment list, wetsuits (or the more expensive dry suit) is a must during cold months. Most people will not paddle during cold seasons but if

Farmer John wetsuit                    Farmer Jane wetsuit

kayaking during the winter calls your name, purchase a wet suit called the Farmer John or Farmer Jane. These resemble overalls.

We do not wear the same type of wetsuit as divers. The full sleeves of diver's wetsuits chafe our armpits after hours of paddling. At a thickness of 2-3 mm you'll stay warm except in extreme cold weather in northern states where 5 mm thickness is recommended. In addition to the wetsuit, purchase wicking fabric, wear layers and absolutely no cotton anything. Cotton is made to keep the skin cool, not warm. On top of the wetsuit, wear a splash jacket. These jackets have a gasket at the neck and wrists, the most vulnerable points of entry for water.

TIP: Wetsuits are unforgiving with regard to size. If your chest is forty inches, purchase a wetsuit made for that size; even if you could zip up a suit made for a thirty-eight inch chest, taking a deep breath would be difficult. Zippers at the ankles is a very nice feature to have.

Note: Some paddlers use the "Rule of 120" to decide whether or not to go out during cold weather. If the combined temperature of the water and air total 120 or more, they paddle. How to find out water temperature? Call an outfitter associated with that waterway. For instance, Google "kayak rental" and type the name of the river. If the sum of the water and air temperature add to less than 120, a wetsuit is necessary.

**Wheels** – Kayak cart for portage.

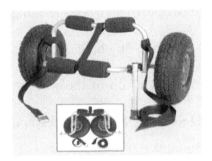 

These cradle one end of the boat – the stern - on foam while the other end of the boat is pulled. When not in use fold the wheels and stash it under the cockpit or deck rigging.

# CHAPTER FIVE

# Basic Strokes

Four movements every paddler learns to get started: Forward, backward, turn and stop. Because learning how to paddle is more by doing than reading, I'll describe strokes and include tips to make your hands-on learning more effective.

First, know where to place your hands on the paddle. Center the paddle on your head and allow your hands to naturally spread out a little past shoulder width to balance it. That is the correct placement – hands a little past shoulder width. For novice paddlers, that is one of the hardest things to remember. During class, one or both of their hands drift closer to the center of the paddle making strokes weak and ineffective. For demonstration, use a shower curtain rod or long stick of wood. Center it on your head and place your hands at slightly past shoulder width, lower it and pretend to paddle. Feel the strength of your movement. Next, slide both hands closer to the center, lower it and again pretend to paddle. You've lost the strength of movement and the ends flop. Now slide your hands slightly past shoulder width and again pretend to paddle. The correct position is your power spot.

Novices and experienced alike tend to allow one hand to drift toward the center of the paddle while maintaining the correct position of the other hand. The result? A boat that keeps pulling to one side and impossible to go straight ahead. If your boat keeps going to the left or right, first check your hand placement. For river and lake paddling, correct hand placement is so critical that some paddlers put waterproof tape on their paddle as a reminder.

Boats pull to one side for another reason. We're all stronger on one side but in some the dominant arm is much stronger. Perhaps there was a past injury on one side and the other side does one and a half times the work. The good news is that kayaking can help strengthen the weak side. What I've found works the best to compensate until the weaker arm strengthens: Do two strokes on the weaker side for each stroke on the dominant side. I've worked with students in the past who attempt to paddle weaker on the strong side and stronger on the weak side. That doesn't work. Instead, do two strokes on the weak side to one stroke on the strong side.

**Tip**: When paddling for the first time, concentrate on proper stroke technique, hand placement and keeping the boat under control rather than speed. Mind and muscles are laying down the foundation for eventually paddling by instinct. If you're on a group paddle, find an experienced paddler who does not have a history of frequent flips and ask them to buddy up with you if the paddle organizer has not already done so. Watch your buddy kayak, mimic them and let them know about any specific problems you encounter with your technique. Ideally, learn from an American Canoe Association certified instructor. Their eye is so well trained that they'll be able to see what you do correctly or incorrectly. The point is that it is best to learn good habits from the first time in the water because once a bad habit is learned, it is difficult to retrain mind and muscles.

Sit up straight and paddle using torso rotation. It allows for longer strokes – feet to seat - and allows the body to engage core musculature. An untrained paddler uses only their arms and shoulders. When students can't isolate turning from the waist, I have them sit on the ground and twist. That works! If your shoulders burn, check that you are sitting up straight and using torso rotation. Consciously tighten the muscles of your abdomen with each stroke. It adds umph to your strokes.

**Going Forward:** Especially if you've paddled a canoe, your instinct directs to more vertical than horizontal paddling. In other words, you will have a tendency to direct the paddle blade close to the side of the boat and at a higher angle when performing a forward stroke. While kayak paddling isn't horizontal, it certainly is more so than canoeing because kayaks sit lower in the water than canoes. In the photos below, note the

higher angle of the canoe oar than the kayakers paddles:

These kayakers hold their
paddles at the perfect
height and angle.

Sit on the floor and pretend that you have a paddle in

your hands. With a slight torso twist, reach the blade forward

dipping the shoulder slightly on that side and pretend to plant it in the water near your feet. Stop. Is your hand above your head? If so, that is the elevated angle of a canoeing paddle position. Lower your hand; the blade naturally extends out more to the side. This is the beginning position of a kayaking forward stroke. Follow through with the draw by twisting your torso from the waist up and stop the paddle just behind your butt. That is as far as the blade should travel until you pull it out of the water to do the same sequence on the other side of the boat. The full length of the stroke is feet to seat. Beginner's make the mistake of putting the paddle in the water at their knees. Stretch forward and set the paddle in the water at your feet. The long strokes make for graceful, effective paddling.

It's worth repeating that if you get wet while paddling, you are lifting the paddle too high. Present a perfectly vertical, flat blade to the water. Not holding it vertically, in other words slicing the blade decreases water resistance resulting in weak and inefficient strokes.

Slicing the blade

Especially when fatigued, paddlers tend to slice. It's best to take a break rather than to keep trying.

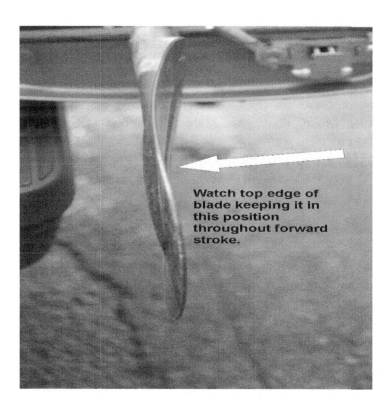

**Watch top edge of blade keeping it in this position throughout forward stroke.**

As mentioned earlier, the power face is scooped. Basic strokes require that the scooped side face the paddler.

After a few paddles, you might experience what I call the "zen" moment. With increased arm muscles and a vertical paddle, the water feels as though it is pushing against the paddle, rather than the paddle pushing against the water. It almost feels as if a hand is gently pushing against the paddle with each stroke. It's hard to imagine but in time I hope you have that zen moment.

There are two methods by which to forward stroke: "Push" and "Pull." Pull utilizes the muscles of one arm to follow through the stroke, Push uses both. Which one is the more efficient stroke and propels a kayak faster? The two-handed Push. We're going to spend a little time discussing both.

**Tip:** The two-handed Push stroke firms up the flabby muscle on the underneath side of the arms. However, if you have wrist or elbow tendonitis, do not do the two-handed push stroke as it aggravates tendonitis.

The Pull Stroke:  Most of us naturally do this stroke. With the left paddle blade in the water at the beginning of the stroke, pull it back with the left arm. The right hand just goes along for the ride lifting the blade into the air. On the reverse side, the right arm does the pulling while the left arm goes along for the ride.

The Push Stroke: Pretend to hold a paddle with the blade submerged in the water on the left side. Open the palm of your right hand against the shaft of the paddle. With almost a punching force, push your right hand straight out from your shoulder while simultaneously pulling with your left hand. Because the resistance of water is required for the blade to stay upright against the right handed open palm, this must be practiced while actually paddling.

Regardless of the push or pull methods, sit up straight, keep the blade vertical and engage the core muscles by rotating the torso when paddling.

**Going Backwards:** Twist toward the back of the boat from your midsection and keep the blade straight up and down. Place the blade into the water close to the boat and as far behind as you can. Push it forward. Repeat on the other side. When paddling, you'll probably do a few on one side and then a few on the other side rather than a pure left/right, left/right. It is important to keep the scoop face in the same position as the forward stroke. A lot of my students tend to flip the blade such that the scoop faces the bow of the boat. If you pull hard enough during a back stroke with the power face facing the bow, there's a chance that you'll capsize.

**Turning:** There are several ways to turn. If river kayaking, the easiest turn is to simply put one blade in the water straight up and down while holding it there allowing the current to do most of the work. Another way turn is to do several forward strokes exclusively on one side. A third way is to perform backward strokes on one side only. The fastest and most effective way to turn is performing a forward stroke on one side and a backward stroke on the other side.

**Tip:** When going around a bend on a river, begin turning your boat sooner rather than later. New paddlers tend to wait until they are already in the bend before turning their boat. Caught in the current, they end up on the far riverbank wondering what just happened. A general rule: The longer the kayak, the sooner you should start the turn.

**Stop that boat:** There are several ways to stop.

Stop and dodge: The boat in front of you suddenly puts it in reverse. It's OK to play bumper boats occasionally on recreational paddles but the current is fast and you'd rather not. Plunge the paddle straight up and down into the water on one side using muscle to force it to stay locked in that position. Holding down the paddle on the left side forces the boat to turn in that direction and gets you out from behind the boat in front of you. Next, do quick, shallow backstrokes on both left and right sides of the boat. Presume that it is prudent that you also avoid whatever caused the paddler in front of you to back away.

Stay in one place mid-current: To go past a strainer, boats must go single file which means staying in place while waiting your turn. If the current is strong for a Class I waterway, a continuing series of mini-back strokes straight out from your waist keeps you in place. If the current is not very strong, simply put the paddle with the blade straight up and down on the right, hold for three seconds and then submerge it on left side, a six second (three on each side) series of flapping the paddle up and down. I call this one butterfly wings.

Quick stop: For a really fast stop, plant the paddle blade close to the kayak by your waist, hesitate for a moment in that position and then submerge it on the other side. Don't elevate the paddle straight up and down nor plant it far from the kayak. The planting site is about midway of a normal stroke. Hold tight to the paddle to keep it in place. The more securely you set the paddle, the more effective it is as a brake. What you are doing is applying pressure against the current your boat produced from your forward paddle strokes; if you've been paddling fast, that's a lot of energy to work against. Caution: Flip the paddle side to side to prevent a capsize. If, after planting the blade on one side, you hold it past the count of three seconds, you'll probably kiss the water. If you hold it less than three seconds, the boat won't stop, it'll just keep sliding forward. The goal on a quick stop is getting the boat to a halt in the same number of feet as the kayak. If you are in a twelve foot kayak, the boat must stop within twelve feet.

Don't slice the blade when you plunge it into the water. You won't stop. Sink the whole blade section of the paddle into the water. If you dip it in partially, again you won't stop. A good quick stop takes commitment, a bit of strength and a lot of determination.

# CHAPTER SIX

# OOPS!

Nothing scares newbies more than capsizing. We cannot eliminate capsizes, but reduce the risk? Yes. In this chapter we'll discuss the most common and innocuous flips to the most dangerous, how to enhance paddling safety, describe a capsize moment by scary moment, and end with river protocols.

Most flips occur getting in and out of a kayak. It's funny but it's true. It happens to even the most experienced kayakers. On one run, a paddler traversed twelve miles uneventfully then flipped at the take-out. Nothing got hurt except his pride.

Kayakers learn from their experience and that of other paddlers with whom they paddle resulting in regional ways of doing things right. To use an analogy, in Florida after a hurricane that knocks out power to red lights, drivers treat each intersection as though it is a four-way stop. No one formally broadcasts that practice; drivers learn it from one another. The same applies to kayaking. In Tennessee, they're called sit-on-stops. In Florida, sit upons. Other ways exist on how to do things, how to enter and exit kayaks for instance.

Here is the sequence I teach students to minimize flips getting into a kayak. Visualize that the kayak is floating in the water at least past the seat. (If the boat is in the water bow to stern, balance is even more essential.) Here's how:

- Place the paddle on the ground next to the boat, dismantle it and put both halves in the kayak or hand it to a buddy. Clear the inside deck – nothing in the cup holder or where your legs will go. Entering must be done in one smooth motion and nothing should impede that or get in the way in case of a slip.

- Crouch down close to the kayak and grab the coaming on either side. Place a foot *in the center* of the kayak in front of the seat. It is important that you plant your foot dead center to maintain balance.

- Quickly and smoothly lower your body and get your butt in the seat. The closer you are to the boat when entering this way, the less chance of the kayak rocking. Hesitation when getting your butt in the seat means, you guessed it, flipping.

- Bring in your other leg.

- Stretch your legs out straight, press your back against the seat and sit up straight. The more evenly your body weight is distributed, the greater the balance.

To recount, the sequence is one leg, butt, and then other leg done in one smooth motion.

To exit:

- When approaching land, paddle hard and fast to launch the kayak on solid ground. Ideal for exiting means three-quarters of the kayak is grounded. At least part of the boat will be in water.

- Plant one foot on the ground.

- *Lean forward* and grab the coaming on both sides of the front of the boat.

- When leaning forward, shift your weight to the leg on the land and exit.

Ask a buddy to hold down or straddle the front or back of the boat until you feel confident getting in and out.

TIP: If flexibility is an issue making it difficult to get in and out of a kayak, enter the take-out backwards. Go in stern first. That way when exiting the boat, you're facing downhill making it much easier to get out.

Getting perched midstream on a log is an immediate flipping opportunity. The worse thing to do is sit still. In almost every scary situation on the river, the absolute worst thing to do is nothing. In the moment while you're thinking about what to do, the boat will make a move. And it's not good. You cannot balance the boat in a precarious situation for long. Hopefully your paddling buds are nearby and can help push your boat off the obstruction or extend their paddle for you to grab while they pull. Regardless, start scooting your hips in a quick series of forward motion as soon as you get stuck. Don't scoot to the side! If you can safely do so without losing balance, stab your paddle against the obstruction to gain purchase while continuing the scooting.

Another point to keep in mind to avoid capsizing – when ducking under branches hanging over the water, lean forward or backward. Never lean to the right or left to dodge something. If you lean to the side, the boat will do exactly what you are telling it to do.

One of the most dangerous situations I've encountered is a boat trapped on a rock ledge that is just under the surface. As soon as you realize your boat is landed on a rock ledge, put one leg outside the boat to push off the rock. If the boat swamps meaning it fills with water, abandon it and get yourself to safety. It's up to the group to assist with ropes and manpower to dislodge it if possible.

Another similar situation is a boat turned sideways to the current against a rock ledge. Again, the boat swamps but even faster than if it was pointing downstream because the broadside is open to the current. Abandon it and swim to safety. Again, rely on paddling buds to rescue your kayak. The order of importance for all rescues: paddler, kayak, equipment.

The most dangerous situation for recreational paddlers is strainers. I've seen a strainer grab hold of a thirty-two-pound, eight feet boat manned by an *experienced* paddler. A boat of such light weight and length was, and is, no match for the strength of that current, and the best argument for a longer, heavier kayak for recreational paddling if you live in an area where strainers form in the rivers. They are life and death situations for recreational paddlers. As strainers grow in size, they pull the current toward them. If you get stuck in that current, you *will* go into the strainer. We call them strainers because water flows through them but we do not.

Strainer on Harpeth River, Nashville, Tennessee

Same strainer after spring flooding

If the rivers are elevated, the only way to safely manage the strainer in the second photo is portaging kayaks. Get to the riverbank upstream of the current rushing into the strainer. However, if you are ever in the unfortunate situation of getting caught in a strainer's current, here's what to do: As the current forces your boat toward the strainer, turn the boat sideways. Do not approach it bow first. This is not the approach for canoes! The goal is to get your body close to the mass of debris. As soon as the boat comes to rest horizontal to the strainer, push down firmly on the hip and leg closest to it. In other words, lean the kayak into the strainer. With the boat dipped down on that side and the side presented to the current raised up, a paddler gains a few lifesaving moments of preventing the water from spilling over the edge of the kayak and into the cockpit.

Reach with both hands and grab some branches in the pile of debris, continue to keep your weight tipped toward the strainer and then hoist yourself up onto the strainer. As your feet make contact, test that it will hold your weight. Do not lean down to grab for anything inside the boat. Nothing – not your cell phone, or car keys - is worth risking your life. Climb up the strainer and scramble off of it to dry land if possible.

What happens next depends on the circumstances – the boat may fold in half from the force of the current – "clamshell" - or get pinned to the strainer. If your buddies are immediately on hand and can safely do so they can attempt to save the boat. An inexpensive kayak capable of bending by hand has no chance, and lessens the paddler's chance, of surviving a strainer. It's important to act quickly because the force of the water may collapse the boat pinning the paddler between the kayak and strainer.

To avoid entrapment in a strainer, keep a vigil eye downriver – bridge pylons frequently amass strainers as do bends. If the strainer lies around the bend you will hear the rushing current. From upriver, it sounds like a waterfall. Presuming that you always paddle with at least one buddy, go single file past it. Others stay in place until the paddler in front of them is past the danger. The first one in safer water past the strainer stays put to be available in case anyone needs help.

A strainer caught me by surprise. On approach the river split left and right with dry land in the middle of the riverbed. There were only two choices – down river left or right. On the side I choose, around the bend lay a strainer that traversed the width of the river. There was no turning back. Upon approach, I turned my boat sideways to the strainer. After the boat came to rest parallel to the strainer, I leaned into the mass of limbs and branches and, abandoning my kayak, climbed up onto them. My buddies were watching, landed their boats on the dry bed in the middle and rescued my boat. It took three men to pass me hand-over-hand from atop the mass of limbs onto dry land.

## Safety Begins Before Wetting a Paddle

Recognize and eliminate factors that contribute to capsizes. Here are several pointers to assist recreational paddlers from taking a swim.

**The right boat length and weight:** Presuming a river with a mild current of two miles per hour, we're going to apply a safety factor method simply called "450." That number is derived by multiplying the kayak's length by its weight. For example, a ten feet, forty-five pounds boat is 450. This minimum baseline for safety does not imply a 450 is 100% safe. Nothing on the river is 100% safe. Numbers greater than 450 increase the boat's safety factor for recreational paddling. The ideal is 540-564.

**Stop when fatigued – better yet, before:** Few opportunities exist for many of us ladies to build upper body strength. Add to that the fact that an untrained beginner's paddling strokes are less efficient and more energy consuming than experienced strokes. The result - weak muscles that are suddenly overworked.

We're independent, self-reliant people conditioned to not show pain yet if your shoulders burn after a couple hours of paddling and it appears that everyone else is fine, trust me, you are not the only one who is hurting. I am grateful, and happy to comply, when an inexperienced paddler asks to take a break.

**Buddies:** Best practice is four paddlers at a minimum. Safety classes teach that in the event of an emergency, one buddy stays with the victim while two buddies go for help. If paddling with a group, staying together is the best safety precaution. If someone lags behind for any reason, ensure a buddy stays with them. Friends do help friends stay upright - it might be a helpful nudge that dislodges your kayak off an obstacle, someone holding onto the kayak as you climb inside or a coach when facing a difficult chute.

**Skill level matches river classification:** He had a lot of experience, it was her first paddle. On a Class II no less. Despite that she was in good shape and athletic, muscles don't substitute for experience. While she caught her breath on the river bank

after her second capsize, he asked his now enraged fiancee',
"Do you still want to marry me?"

Do not let anyone talk you into a run that sounds too
difficult for your ability. If your paddle leader states that
paddlers must have experience for a particular run, please
respect that advice. Attending a paddle beyond your experience
endangers yourself *and* the group. Organizer, it is kinder to send
someone home if you believe their experience is subpar for a
particular run than to allow them to attend.

A good question is, when to amp up from Class I to
Class II paddling? The quick answer is experience. The more
complete answer is *recent* experience which interprets to ability
plus muscles. If paddling regularly with a group, check with the
organizer for their opinion and ask for a buddy if you get a green
light. If your paddling history includes gaps of time, rebuild
paddling muscles on a few Class I runs before attempting Class
II.

**Know the condition of the run:** Those earthquakes in
California, summertime hurricanes in Florida or heavy rains

during springtime in Tennessee alter the landscape of our waterways. Ask experienced paddlers or that river's outfitter. They'll tell you where to go, what to look out for and what changed on the river. If you just can't wait to get started, head out to more open bodies of water such as a lake and always take a buddy. I know some people do it but I still preach: Never paddle alone.

**Alcohol:** Kayaking + alcohol = capsize. It's not a good idea for *anyone* to drink and paddle. Save it for after the paddle.

**Match the speed of the kayak to that of the current:** When the river channel narrows or bends, the speed of the current increases dramatically. To maintain control of the kayak, start paddling hard and fast. Dig in! I've watched many newbs panic, and stop paddling. As mentioned previously, stopping paddling is the worst thing to do because when you freeze, the current grabs hold of the kayak and takes it where *it* wants to go. It's an out-of-control situation. Organizer, this is the time to make your voice heard. Coach that panic-struck paddler – call their name and assertively order them to paddle. Keep it short and simple:

"Kyle, get your paddle in the water! Paddle!" Especially when rounding a bend with a strong current, paddle hard. If you don't, the current may grab hold of the kayak, shove it against the riverbank and flip it. When you learn how to paddle using your lower body in addition to the upper, you won't have to paddle so hard and fast when the current speed increases.

**Keep the boat pointing straight downstream:** The best position for going downstream is the front of the boat pointing downstream. Sounds obvious, and it is, but at times even a Class I current pushes a boat sideways. The kayak is broached. If a kayak gets turned sideways, that is the front and back point toward the riverbanks rather than up- and downstream, the kayak becomes a dam, fills with water and flips. If the flow is turbulent, *as soon as* you feel it pulling your boat sideways dig in with all the muscles you've got and fight to keep the bow pointing downstream.

**It's not always best to flow with the current:** If the current is relatively swift, such as after a recent downpour, bends become trickier to navigate. Going with the current under these circumstances is a poor choice.

 In this picture notice the current pulling toward the small strainer on the left. To paddle with the current in this case, the boat would be pulled into the strainer, even as small as it is. Instead, follow the path as indicated with the arrow cutting across the current and then into the calmer section called the "eddy."

Generally, if the river bends to the left paddle to the right of mid-river. Conversely, if the river bends to the right, paddle to the left of mid-river. With an S curve, paddle straight down the middle. It takes muscle!

### Oops!

No capsize is to be taken lightly but the worst that happens during the course of most recreational runs is that the paddler gets soaked and we rodeo the boat and gear. This in no way makes light of a life and death situation such as getting pinned to a strainer. No inexperienced paddler should be on a river that presents such extreme danger.

For the type of waterways on which you'll learn, it is most likely you or a paddle mate will have a situation like this one: It happened so fast it felt like someone grabbed the side of your boat and pulled down hard. There is no mistaking the sound of someone capsizing on the river and, if your organizer did their job, assigned rescuers are on their way. Until they reach you, as obvious as it sounds, come out from under the boat and come up for air. A newbie once panicked to such an extent that I had to lift her boat from on top of her and pull her up. She didn't swallow any water but we sat on the riverbank until she breathed normal and calmed down. You have no idea how you are going to react when you panic! After you are on top of the water, if you can grab your boat, do so. If the water is shallow and the current is slow, stand up and walk out. If the water is deep and a fast current, float on your back. Extend your legs with your toes pointed downstream and blow three long blasts on the whistle attached to your life jacket.

I've asked kayakers what is their first thought when they capsize. Their answer: To grab onto their boat. That makes sense, to desire grabbing onto something that floats and that is the ACA's recommendation. Grab your boat and either hold on to the back of it or wrap your legs around the stern. What happens on rec paddles is that the boat floats downstream before there's a chance to grab it. If the boat floated downstream before you could grab it, start swimming for the closest land. The goal is to get you out of the water as soon as possible.

Again, if the kayak floated away, the river is deep and the current is strong, stay with your toes pointed downstream and float. Your life jacket keeps your head above water. One of the rescuers throws a rope. Grab it, hold on and let them pull you to safety. Rescuers, do not jump in the water unless it is absolutely necessary to save a life. The ACA teaches that anyone in the water is a victim. Staying in your boat keeps you in a stronger position to assist.

Finally, you are out of the water and safe.

What happens next: Paddle buddies retrieve your boat and anything they can safely grab that's floating. That is why a bright colored dry bag is so important. Some paddlers use a carabiner to clip the dry bag to the boat. While you catch your breath and calm down, others empty the kayak of water or, if you need to move and the swamped boat is nearby, assist with emptying it. That is why it's best to purchase a kayak with a drain plug. A kayak filled with water is heavy!

Trip leader, blow three long blasts on the whistle even if the capsize hasn't yet occurred but is definitely imminent. Your first priority is the paddler in the water; let others tend to the kayak and gear. If you have not participated in rescues, practice rescues under non-emergency situations. Practicing your first rescue during an emergency is not a wise thing to do.

Resist the urge, and discourage everyone, from flipping the boat upright mid-river to pull it to land. Water weighs seven pounds per gallon and a swamped rec boat weighs, well, a lot. It's my experience that helpful paddlers who upright a kayak mid-river, tie it with a rope to their boat get flipped by the sloshing water and weight of the swamped kayak. Instead, leave the kayak upside down. A rescuer butts the bow of their kayak against the flipped one's middle and nudges the flipped boat to dry land. It's called, "bulldozing." If the boat is too long for one kayaker to bulldoze, switch to two rescuers - one butts the bow and the other the stern. Once the boat is near the shore, tilt the kayak to drain the water. Tilt it higher and higher as the water drains until it is empty enough to be pulled up onto land.

It is critical that paddles have one, and only one, leader. Chaos and panic during a capsize make it difficult for people to think clearly. Some withdraw and get quiet, some spring to action at the first sign of trouble, some wait and do what they are told to do. It is your voice that they have keyed into from the pre-paddle talk and it is your voice that stays calm and assertive.

After a capsize, I pull the group over for a break during which I visit with each person one-on-one. Sometimes a capsize aftereffect is shock – surprisingly, it may be ones who watched it happen. I ask each person how they are. Do they make eye

contact and what is the look on their face? Assess skin color –
normal, pale, splotchy? Are they talking normally, stuttering, or
worse, not talking? Some get surprised or embarrassed by their
reaction. Inject some humor if it is not inappropriate.

In my experience, as stated earlier in this chapter, most
rec capsizes result in *non-traumatic* capsizes meaning people
and boats come out in one piece. Hope for the best but please
always be prepared for the worst. Group leaders, take a river
safety course, get CPR certified and have previous experience
with rescues before leading groups.


### River Protocols and Courtesies

As with biking or driving a car, kayaking has its own
protocols. Some are rules and some are courtesies shared
paddler to paddler.

- At the put-in, everyone stays in place in the water until
  the last paddler is in the water, too.

- If you encounter paddlers coming upstream while you
  are traveling downstream, honor the same protocol as

that of the roads. In America, downstreamers to the right, upstreamers to the left.

- It is no secret that kayaks go faster than canoes. Most canoeists do us the courtesy of allowing us to pass them. If they don't it's OK to get around them. I once heard from a couple canoeists, "That does it. Next time we rent kayaks."

- When the Point uses a Universal River Signal, paddlers convey it to those behind them until the message reaches the Sweep.

- If someone encounters a potential danger such as a log barely under the surface, they tell the paddlers behind them. Again, the information is conveyed through the remainder of the group downstream until it reaches the Sweep.

- At lunch break, I use humor to help everyone figure out which way to go to go: "Men to the left, women to the right because women are always right."

- When launching after a break, leave nothing behind but footprints.

- If lake paddling, paddle in the motor boat section and do not paddle in areas designated for swimmers. When crossing a lake occupied with motorboats, stay close together for several reasons. It makes you easier to spot, gives the motorboats less to dodge and keeps you close enough to respond if someone flips.

- During rescues, hopefully there is enough communication such that members waiting it out down river know what is happening. If you are one of those waiting, please know that some rescues take a while and you are doing the right thing waiting it out.

- Hug, or at least rub the arms of, someone who flipped and stay with them until their breathing is normal. If they came up laughing, they don't need this extra care. The organizer, or one of the stronger paddlers, should buddy up with that person for a while after getting back in the water even if they shrugged it off like it was nothing.

- Tell your group leader if you have special needs.

- If you are fishing or taking pictures, it is your responsibility to catch up with the group.

- It's a personal choice but I discourage paddlers from photographing capsizes. If you do take them, though, as a courtesy before putting photos where they are available to everyone (like bosses and coworkers) please ask the photo subject. Most people are good sports about it but it's not anyone's diva moment.

- Cell phone usage detracts from the enjoyment of the day. Take a few hours to enjoy nature and mute it.

- Huge controversy going on about music playing during a paddle. I put it in the same category as cell phones; guess that tells you where I stand. Not everyone shares the same taste in music and when it's playing, there's no getting away from it. If you're out with only your buddies, that's one thing but if you're with a group, be courteous and don't force others to listen to your music.

# CHAPTER SEVEN

# How to Transport a Kayak

This is a *huge* deal, especially for women. And understandably so. I've met only two women in twenty years capable of lifting a kayak over their head to put it on J racks. The rest of us just don't have the right muscles for overhead lifting. When I led group paddles, I learned that a lot of women bought kayaks based on its weight which means they bought ten-foot boats. They'd take those inappropriate kayaks on the river and have a miserable time. Boats that length don't track very well unless you know how to manage it and, in strong Class I currents, the kayak lacked the weight of a twelve-footer needed to maintain control. I applaud these determined ladies and, in this chapter, take the work out of transporting a longer and heavy kayak.

For starters – this is very tongue-in cheek - here's an amusing option for convertible owners:

Jessica Ely, photo by Leslie Dunn

If your kayak is no longer than ten feet, carry that puppy in your passenger seat. When drivers and people along the road stare, extend your fingers, press them up against each other, raise your hand in the air and gently wave it back and forth in the Queen Elizabeth wave and smile.

For one person to load a kayak on top of a car, a secured rack on the car's roof is essential. If you have factory racks, cover them with foam (children's noodles, yoga map, pipe insulation) secured with bungee cords or zip ties – anything that the kayak can sink down into to stay put.

, These are available at sporting goods stores – they're foam pads that fit on car racks. Again, zip tie them to the rack or use bungee cords.

This is another inexpensive option. Not very durable but will get you started.

If you decide that kayaking is your thing, consider a more permanent transport solution. Get racks that are rustproof and durable. They're a bit costly but last for years. Good quality ones do not have to be removed when going through most carwashes and have keys to lock them down so they're theftproof. J-shaped rack systems are popular but these require that the boat be lifted overhead to be cradled inside the crook of the upright J and are not recommended for women.

If your vehicle comes equipped with racks, purchase saddles (also called "boots").

If your car doesn't have a rack, entire rack systems are available that include saddles. Before you buy online, ask a local sporting goods store what they charge for installation because they aren't the easiest thing to put together.

Following is a description of how I loaded a twelve-foot kayak on top of a compact car for years without breaking a sweat: Pull the boat such that the bow is lined up and just under the middle of the back fender. Put a towel or blanket on the back of the trunk. Using the built-in handle of the boat, pick up the bow and rest it on the top of the towel-covered trunk. During the loading process – great news! – you are already done with all the lifting that is required.

Photo by Jay A. Heath, Ed.D

Next, walk to the stern and with a steady push, slide the boat first past the rear window and then in between the saddles, or on top of the protective device you use, centering the kayak over the length of the car. Walk a little distance away from the car to judge whether or not it is truly centered.

Sterns are heavier than the bow to explain why it is loaded with the bow toward the front of the car.

Unloading the boat is as simple as loading. Put the towel or blanket in the middle of the trunk. Unstrap the kayak and give it a tug to get it started. Guide the kayak as it slides down the back of the car. The maximum size recommended, especially if your car is a compact, is 14'. Some paddlers transport their boat upside down, something with which I disagree. If the boat is of sufficient thickness, transporting it right side up will not damage the boat. In fact, strapping it down upside down can "oilcan" the boat – it gets a permanent indentation, meaning it buckles from the tension of the strap – and that dent is impossible to remove and ruins the kayak.

Next, how to strap it down. From this point forward, there will be two sets of instructions – one for rack owners and one for those without a rack. For rack owners: A variety of straps are available. I use the 2" cam straps with a slide through clasp buckle on the end. They come in a variety of colors.

Photo courtesy of David Quist Photography
and Strapworks.com

There is another kind of strap with cinches that rachet down. I strongly recommend not using these as they easily oilcan a boat because they do not stop when they are tight enough. You can keep ratcheting and ratcheting without realizing the kayak is buckling. The straps above that I recommend stop when they are tight and will not harm the boat.

Open the driver's door and step up onto the car facing the car. With one end of the strap in hand, loop it through the metal rod of the rack and toss both ends of the strap all the way over the boat to the opposite side of the car. When tossing, be careful with the buckle and the windows. Two straps go on the boat – one in front of the cockpit and one behind it. Open the back door, step onto the car and repeat the process. If utilizing foam blocks with no rack system, follow these same directions.

Walk around to the other side of the car. Grasp the end of the strap that does not have the clasp and loop it around the metal rod on the rack. Thread this same end through the clasp:

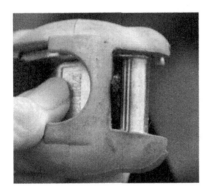 

Repeat the process with the strap around the back part of the kayak. This time, pull down using both hands to get that strap as snug as you can make it. Go back to the first one and see if it will now tighten down any further.

Next, turn the buckle upside down and wrap the end of the strap around the rest of the strap three times.

Insert the end of the strap through the loop closest to the buckle. Starting at the top, slide the trio of loops toward the buckle and repeat this process twice.

The end piece was

shortened in these photographs for demonstration. When the boat is secured and unmovable, place the end piece in the open door and close the door or trim the straps to the length that's needed so there's no overhang.

Last, grab the side of the kayak and give it a good shake. It should not move independent of the car. If it moves, you must tighten the straps. Any movement of the boat must be eliminated even if it means undoing the knots and pulling down harder on the straps.

What to do with any extra length of strap hanging down? Tuck it inside the open door and shut the door, trim it or keep wrapping it around the taut strap.

Without a rack and using foam blocks or some other type of cushioning device, there's nothing to hook the straps around so there's a different process. Toss the ends of the straps without the buckle over the kayak. Climb over the backseat and pull the strap through the inside of the car. Pull the ends of the straps through the buckles and yank them as tight as possible. Step out of the car and pull if necessary. See the above description for knotting it. For safety, grab the kayak and try to move it. If the car shakes when you move the kayak, you're good to go. It's got to be that tight!

For added protection, tie down the bow and stern of the kayak through the handles to underneath the front end of the car and under the trunk. Both ropes must be as taut as possible. I've never done this in twenty years but, as I say during the lesson, if

it makes you feel safer, do it. Also, some folks tie down the
front of the kayak to both the right and left front of the car, like
an inverted "V" like the second car in the picture:

When paddling with others, watch how they load and
strap their boats down. Some even have racks that crank up and

down with a long bar that swivels down horizontally to the middle of the windows. The boat is placed on that long bar and then cranked up to the roof. This is the least labor intensive but most expensive system.

As with learning anything new, the first few times you load your boat allow yourself plenty of time so that you arrive on time for the paddle. Or load it the night before.

# CHAPTER EIGHT

# How To Organize and Lead a Group Paddle

This chapter seems off topic but it is included for Scouts, church groups or anyone who wants to lead a group paddle. There is no book that I could find with this information. We don't know what we don't know and sometimes we don't even know the questions to ask. In this chapter, you'll find detailed instructions for preplanning, in addition to what to do and take for, a well-organized, fun and safe kayak excursion.

You are the organizer and today is the day of a shuttled paddle. The twenty attendees are a mixture of ages and levels of kayaking experience. It is summer, the forecast indicates no rain verified with a last-minute check, and everyone borrowed, rented or owns a boat. We'll go over details that led to this moment, followed by those that follow it.

Note: Some of the details may not make sense in the moment that you read it but, as continue through the chapter, the details will become clear. For the following paddle scenario, let's presume that the organizer is experienced and that there is a pre-appointed safety person who knows Universal River Safety Signals (which will be discussed in this chapter).


**Before the Day of the Paddle**

Mr. or Ms. Organizer, you've chosen to paddle on a river with which you are familiar and you know that it's a Class I. Several attendees have zero experience so rather than a ten mile stretch you'd choose for a group with experience under their paddles, you choose to do a six mile run. I strongly recommend that inexperienced paddlers do no more than six miles their first couple times. If the group is all children, then you'd plan a three or four mile trip but today's group is adults. Given an average rate of speed downstream at two miles per hour, add an extra half-hour for lunch and another half-hour for breaks. This calculates to four hours of river time. With a group this large, and that this is a shuttled paddle, add another hour for getting cars and boats where they need to be.

Normal put-in locations are riverbanks and bridges and these have no physical address. To avoid lost drivers, choose a brick and mortar physical location near the put-in at which to meet. For today's paddle, that location is a gas station.

TIP: Some people travel by cell phone navigation, some use satellite navigators and others by written directions. Posting the address of the gas station takes care of those traveling by personal devices. When advertising the event, include a detailed list of roads and turns for those who travel by printed description. Warning: Many cell phones lose connectivity near the rivers which is another good reason to meet at a physical location.

Unless the put-in and take-out are familiar, before the day of the paddle drive from the gas station to the put-in and then to the take-out making note of the length of driving time and miles. Scan the parking lot at the take-out ensuring that it can accommodate the number of cars.

One of the most frequent questions asked of a paddle organizer is, "Do you know what time we will get back?" There is only one correct answer: No. In my experience, behind that question is someone who needs to get back home on time to do something later in the day. There's an old saying that applies – you can plan the event, but not the outcome. Your paddle today may be uneventful or full of surprises. That's what makes each paddle an adventure!

If there is any question about the quality of the run – perhaps it stormed a few days ago – check on the internet if an outfitter is available that services the river. Use "kayak rental" and the name of the river as search terms. Another resource is that river's governmental water management organization. Did the recent storm knock down trees? What is the current today? If early in the season, ask for the water temperature. Also, get the number of the county or closest city's emergency medical professionals and store it in your cell phone. While you are preplanning, ensure that you have cell phone service near the river. If not, set a back-up plan for contacting an emergency service while paddling

My group members sign releases on which they note their emergency contact. Most of my paddlers are frequent flyers; at home I maintain a spreadsheet of each one's emergency contact. A hard copy of that list gets tucked inside a plastic bag and stored in my drybag. Ask everyone with a cell phone to store an ICE (In Case of Emergency) number. If their phone is password protected, ask them to remove the protection for the day of the paddle or doublecheck the spreadsheet for their emergency contact.

Share your phone number with each attendee.

Request that every paddler bring: A change of clothing in a sealed plastic bag, lots of water (no alcohol), snacks and lunch, sunscreen, hat, sunglasses, bug spray, whistle, first aid kit, medical alert/medications/special need items. Please note: Ask anyone with special needs to please share that information with you privately.

Another frequently asked question is what to wear on a paddle. So much depends upon where you live, the season and time of the day. I answer in only the broadest terms. If it's a spring or fall paddle and early in the day, wear layers – jacket, thick button up shirt, T-shirt. Any type of wicking garment works, whether it is pants and/or shirt. I prefer wicking pants that either roll up or snap to convert into shorts. In the summer, cotton is king.

I disagree with the popular idea of wearing wicking clothing during the summer. Think of it in the most basic sense – our bodies sweat to keep us cool when we're hot. Wearing clothing that absorbs the sweat with quick drying fabric runs counter to our natural cooling system. On the other hand, cotton retains moisture and stays damp therefore doubling the cooling action of perspiration. The correct time, in my opinion, to wear wicking material is when we need to stay dry – during cold months.

Given the nature of the sport of continuously sitting in an upright position, to avoid a paddler tan on your legs use sunscreen and re-apply after getting wet. Otherwise, the front half gets bronzed while the back half is in the shade.

## The Day of the Paddle

Ensure that your cell phone is fully charged. Keep it close because you *will* get last minute calls. Load up and head out early enough to ensure you are the first one to arrive. If you aren't there when people start to arrive, they get anxious about whether or not you are going to show up. Sounds silly but it is true. You asked everyone to meet at the gas station at 9:00 a.m. It's now 9 a.m. but one person is missing. What happens next is up to you, and here are my guidelines: If I do a headcount and someone hasn't arrived and hasn't called, at 9:05 we caravan to the put-in. You may think, *Only five minutes?* When you ask an excited group who all managed to get there on time to wait for one late person, each minute feels like ten. If the late comer calls saying that they are stuck in traffic, I wait a reasonable amount of time. What is reasonable? My choice is if, by 9:30 they have not arrived, I call them with directions to the put-in and head out. Sometimes organizers have to make tough calls.

Lead the cars to the put-in. Remember not all drivers are speed demons, which is tongue in cheek for saying that some drivers rarely go over 45 mph. It's better to go a little slower and not lose anyone. Hopefully the jaunt to the water does not include many turns or red lights. If so, be especially cautious. You may want to assign a driver to bring up the rear; swap phone numbers so the two of you can stay in touch in case of slow poke stragglers or someone makes a wrong turn.

It's my personal preference against caravanning cars on the highway. I found it too dangerous for drivers who, in order to keep up with the group, weave in and out of traffic. If you choose to highway caravan, give hard copy directions to each driver.

After everyone arrives at the put-in, it's important that everyone helps each other unload boats and gear. The idea behind this goes beyond basic courtesy. It begins setting the attitude among the group of taking care of each other.

After everyone is done unloading, and before anyone gets in their boat, it's time for the pre-paddle talk. Gather them in a group, and try to ensure that all are present. Sometimes it is like herding cats – they are ready to hit the water but do your best. Introduce yourself to the group and thank them for coming. Ask everyone to state their name for three reasons - it makes for a better day when participants know the names of the others with whom they paddle alongside, it helps break the ice for those who are shy, and if the worst happens (a capsize) knowing names assists with communication.

Especially for the sake of the newbies, here are the things to cover while everyone is rounded up together:

- Briefly mention the highlights of today's paddle – river classification, length of paddle, stop for lunch on the riverbank, and any interesting things you'll pass on the river such as a waterfall, unique rock formations or animals.

- Safety – If one is pre-selected, introduce the safety person who explains that often we cannot hear each other on the waterways and that is why we use Universal River Safety signals to communicate:

If the Point (or anyone) raises their paddle and points to the right, the group is to paddle to the right side of the river. If someone directs to the left, go to left. Emphasize that the direction in which the paddler is pointing is the direction to go. Any communication from the Point must be sent back through the paddlers until the message reaches the Sweep. This goes for all the following as well.

Waving an upraised paddle three times side to side, or three long blasts on the whistle means emergency.

Raising a horizontal paddle or both arms extended waving three

times means, "Stop now!"

If someone points their paddle straight up it means go down the

middle of the waterway. It also means, "All clear!"

If a paddler makes eye contact with another paddler, pats their head and points at them, it conveys, "Are you all right?" To indicate that all is OK, the other paddler pats their head in response and points back. If there is no response, initiate an emergency response.

If leading a group of children, turn learning these signals into a game: Line them up one behind the other and as the point conveys various signals, the children act them out.

- Now for the scary part. Ask for two experienced paddlers to volunteer to be designated rescuers. Explain to the group, and be emphatic, that in the event of a capsize you (presuming you are the Point), the Sweep and the two designated rescuers will be the only ones to swoop to the rescue. All other paddlers should clear the area and stop along the riverbank to wait until all is clear. Instruct them to retrieve personal items floating downstream if they can safely do so. Capsizes are not a rare occurrence and its best that everyone knows beforehand what to do.

- Assign the Sweep paddler. I recommend bringing waterproof walkie-talkies; they go into the hands of the Point and Sweep. Often, canoeists attend paddles with kayakers. If an experienced canoeist attends, ask them to do Point. Canoes sit higher up in the water for better advantage to see logs just under the water as well as a better view of what is downstream. Your strongest and most experienced paddler is the Sweep. Whether conveyed with humor or strong warning, emphasize to the group that it is their job to stay between the Point and Sweep.

Note: The Point kayaker stops progression down river if the group gets split. Staying together is that important. If the group continues to split, pull everyone over to give slower paddlers time to catch up and take a break.

- Ask newbies to identify themselves. Either ask experienced paddlers to buddy up one-on-one with a newb or assign buddies. On every paddle I've organized, experienced paddlers have stepped up to the plate, bless their hearts.

TIP: If today's paddle includes more newbies than experienced paddlers, before heading down river take a few moments and get everyone in the water for a paddling lesson at as small a ratio as possible of experienced paddlers to newbies. If there are twenty newbs on today's event and five experienced paddlers, assign four newbs per experienced paddler to teach the basic four strokes: forwards, backwards, turns and stop.

Last piece of the pre-paddle talk: Ask who drives the largest vehicles and, of these drivers, if they'd be willing to shuttle drivers from the take-out back to the put-in. Again, every paddle I've organized results in generous offers to assist. With a group of twenty, two to three vehicles are needed to return drivers to the put-in. Request that all the other drivers to please give these two or three volunteers a couple bucks for gas.

Passengers stay with the boats at the put-in while drivers follow each other to the take-out. It's worth mentioning to the passengers that they should not put their kayak in the water until you return. At the take-out everyone parks their car and then pile into the largest vehicles to transport drivers back to the put-in. At the end of the paddle, someone drives these volunteer drivers and their kayaks back to the put-in to retrieve their vehicles.

TIP: After everyone parks at the take-out, and before driving off for the put-in, do a key check, meaning ask the drivers to double check that they have their car keys.

Note: Many paddlers prefer to drive first to the take-out, place boats onto the largest vehicles and return boats and paddlers to the put-in. That means time-consuming work of removing the kayaks from everyone's cars at the take-out and reloading them on bigger vehicles. I think it's easier to transport drivers only and not boats from the take-out to the put-in.

## Things an Organizer Must Have on Hand

In addition to the items mentioned previously such as sunscreen, water, etc. organizers must carry additional equipment and supplies. Everyone should have their own first aid kit but the truth is they don't. Make sure yours is stocked and that the case is waterproof. There are marine first aid kits available for purchase.

I carry oral and topical Benadryl in my drybag. Realizing that oral Benadryl makes one sleepy, don't hesitate to administer it if the allergic reaction is extreme. If hives break out around the victim's neck and face or their tongue swells, administer the liquid Benadryl immediately.

Hand sanitizer comes in small containers and is invaluable if needed. Don't depend on dipping your hands in the river to get them clean.

Sporting good stores sell ropes specifically for water rescues. On paddles, ensure that five of you have a safety throw rope – the  Point, Sweep, two rescuers and yourself, and know how to use it. Practice on dry land. When throwing it to someone who capsized, toss the bag slightly upriver of the swimmer and allow the current to drag the rope to the person. Always dry the rope after the paddle.

I keep a regular piece of rope tied to the handle on the back of my kayak; attached to the rope is a big hook. It's been used to latch my boat into the crevice of a rock mid-river during a rescue, to secure the kayak to a branch on the side of the river while I threw a safety rope and to hook my boat to another one to pull it out of a jam.

As mentioned previously, purchase at least one set of good walkie talkies. For larger groups, purchase two sets. Of note: Before the paddle, ensure that all the radios are set to the same channel and subchannel. Cell phones do not always work on the river and the walkie talkies may be your only means of communication. Carry extra batteries, too.

Available at most drugstores are instant freeze packs, great thing to have on hand for injuries. With a hard whack, the inside container pops open and freezes the contents. Conversely for winter paddles, carry instant warmth packs for hands, toes and feet. For more information on what to do for hypothermia, please research the subject or, even better, take a first aid class.

It's a good idea to carry an emergency blanket no matter what the season or where you live. These are no more than a large, thin sheet of shiny metal-coated plastic about the size of a shower curtain, yet fold up tightly in a plastic sleeve that requires very little space. I've seen paddlers make it through a capsize with a late reaction of shock. Wrapped up in the blanket, it reflects their body heat back to them. A new paddler traumatized by witnessing a capsize should be watched carefully for shock, too.

Other things I carry for a day trip: Extra water, rope, glucose tablets, spare life jacket and a snake bite kit.

**Voice of Experience**

If you plan to lead paddles, take a Wilderness First Aid and CPR class. Not only does it empower you with the knowledge of what to do during an emergency, the additional layers of safety inspire confidence among the group.

Many capsizes result from a lack of confidence, meaning it is possible for a paddler to lose heart in their abilities and permit a capsize to happen. I am not suggesting that capsizes can be avoided simply by paddlers talking themselves out of it;

it often occurs in an instant. But there will be instances where capsizes can be fought against successfully. A paddler's confidence in themselves, their organizer and the group provide one more element of safety.

It is not a question of whether or not a kayaker will capsize. It is a question of when. Some paddlers say we are all between swims. An organizer, however, will be held to a higher standard by the group. Do not lead paddles if you are a frequent swimmer. It is not amusing for the leader to be the one who needs the most rescues on a run and it could be downright dangerous. The group needs to know they are in the hands of a competent paddler.

There seems to be some sort of group psychology that when one person flips, in that moment others follow suit. I've had as many as seven boats flip at one time. Organizer, you must have the ability to stay calm in an emergency; nothing contributes to that ability as much as experience. Please do not begin your kayaking years as a group leader. Move up through the ranks much like any other life event that requires skill. First be a proficient, strong paddler and volunteer to Point, Sweep or assist as a rescuer. After that, lead small groups and build to larger ones.

Emphasize to the group that in the event of an emergency, there will be only one voice of authority – yours. Fear deafens people. Stay assertive. During moments of panic and confusion, it can help save someone's life.

Of all the unpredictable events that occur on a paddle, organizers can influence one of the root – and predictable - causes of many capsizes: fatigue. Watch for these signs:

- Someone asks how much further, and keeps asking.

- A paddler suddenly starts complaining that their boat keeps going either to the right or left. It probably means their arms are giving out.

- A paddler falls behind. I had a paddler who insisted she preferred to paddle slow. There really are paddlers who prefer a slower pace but before this particular lady kept falling behind, she'd kept up with the group. Her sudden change of 'preference' concerned me. I learned how far people will go to not be, what they believe to be, a bother. We switched boats. It was her bad tracking kayak that was wearing her out.

- Inefficient and weak strokes, different from earlier ones.

- The paddler's body starts rocking forward and backward with each stroke as if they were rowing. It means they are attempting to utilize the rest of their body to compensate for depleted arm strength.

- A couple miles into a run, many paddlers fall into a pleasant and serene paddling "zone." However, if someone becomes quiet with a facial expression of grimacing or intense concentration, they are fatigued.

- The most obvious – someone keeps complaining about being sore.

Cognizant that what happens to one happens to everybody on a paddle, if even one person shows signs of fatigue, pull the group over for a break. Odds are that if "only" one person is fatigued, others are, too. If I suspect that the reason for fatigue lies more in the mediocre quality of the boat rather than lack of strength, I switch boats with that paddler. Words cannot describe the difference between paddling a quality vs inferior kayak. This is not kayak snobbery. It's a fact.

As mentioned, some folks truly prefer paddling slow. For them, paddling is more about getting away from it all than a form of exercise. Rather than hold back the whole group, I let them lag behind as long as that slow paddler has a buddy. When I reach the take-out I note the time, and then wait for my cruisers. As organizers, it is our responsibility to ensure that everyone is accounted for at the take-out. If your group is of sufficient size, plan separate runs for cruisers and faster paddlers. Another option is a start time, for example, at nine o'clock for cruisers and ten o'clock for the faster paddlers with an organizer, Point, Sweep and designated safety paddlers for each group.

Unless the current or river geology will not allow for pulling over, we always stop for lunch. It gives everyone time to stretch their legs and take a pit stop. If someone needs a pit stop during the run, ask someone to buddy up with them and move the group slowly downstream until they catch up.

Drinking alcohol during a run is a sensitive subject. Even though I do not allow drinking on my paddles, adults imbibe without permission. The danger lies not only in an impaired ability to act quickly and appropriately, each one of us relies on everyone else whether to give a heads up about a submerged log, scoop up floating belongings after a flip or to blow three whistle blasts on someone's behalf. It is important for me to know I can rely on you, that you are sober and in control of your boat. If the problem persists, as organizers we have the right to say who is and who is not allowed on a paddle.

I don't know if it is the influence of leaders that set the tone, or the result of similar traits among water lovers but the camaraderie is one of the reasons I love kayaking with a group. I watch kayakers hand another one their paddle after they climb in their kayak and give them a push off the riverbank. A few times, someone paddled up to me to quietly let me know that another paddler seems tired. If someone is standing around while others need assistance, ask them to help. Keep alive the sense of taking care of each other first planted when unloading boats and gear at the put-in. It is especially vital during times of need. The group must understand through words and action that they are dependent on each other until the end of the run. Discourage Lone Rangers paddlers who gallop off from the starting gate and are never seen again. Again, you have the authority to decide who can, or cannot, attend your paddles.

Special note about children: For their first couple times out, they think that it is fun to play bumper boats. If the parents don't stop it, the organizer needs to speak up. On the other hand, I've seen an experienced eight-year-old past the game playing phase and paddling with her is a joy. As good as she paddles, though, we keep a close eye on her when the water gets challenging. If I were a group leader of children, I'd discourage them from banging each other's boats until lunch time and then let them play. Enjoy your lunch while keeping a close eye on them while they play, but remember emptying boats is hard work. If the children let the boats flip, let them help empty them.

At the end of the paddle and everyone's kayak is loaded, gear in the cars and final goodbyes are said, do not leave the parking lot until you are certain that everyone's car starts and they're on their way home. After the paddle, some groups meet at a restaurant. To be honest, by the time I'm done, I just want to get home and take a shower. The choice is entirely yours. If you opt to meet at a restaurant, get a headcount and please do the restaurant a favor and call ahead alerting them to the group of rowdy paddlers about to show up. Better yet, if you are leading a group and know beforehand that a number of the paddlers want to meet at a restaurant after the paddle, call a couple days ahead to give the restaurant time to call in extra staff. And please encourage your group to tip generously. Not only does it help your group leave a good impression, it also helps the paddling community at large develop and/or maintain a good reputation.

## ABOUT THE AUTHOR

Leslie Dunn has kayaked for over twenty years and an American Canoe Association certified instructor for twelve. She's taught over 2,500 people learn how to kayak. She's also written for several newspapers and magazines. She lives in Castalian Springs, TN.

Made in the USA
Monee, IL
25 April 2021

66287322R00085